AF454258

ODISHA

A STATE STUDY GUIDE

DEVKI MONDAL

HAWK PRESS

Published by

Hawk Press
4836/24, Ansari Road, Daryaganj
New Delhi – 110 002
Phones: 91-11-23278618, 91-11-43667199
E-mail: thehawkpress@gmail.com
www.thehawkpress.com

Preface

Odisha is one of the 29 states of India. Located in eastern India, it is surrounded by the states of West Bengal to the north-east, Jharkhand to the north, Chhattisgarh to the west and north-west, and Andhra Pradesh to the south. Odisha has 485 kilometres (301 mi) of coastline along the Bay of Bengal on its east, from Balasore to Ganjam. It is the 9th largest state by area, and the 11th largest by population. It is also the 3rd most populous state of India in terms of tribal population. Odia (formerly known as Oriya) is the official and most widely spoken language, spoken by 33.2 million according to the 2001 Census.

All states in India are governed by a parliamentary system of government based on universal adult franchise. India's parliament is bicameral. The lower house is called the Lok Sabha. Odisha contributes 21 members to Lok Sabha. They are directly elected by the electorates. The upper house is called the Rajya Sabha. Odisha contributes 10 members to Rajya Sabha. They are elected by the state's legislature.

The ancient kingdom of Kalinga, which was invaded by the Mauryan emperor Ashoka in 261 BCE resulting in the Kalinga War, coincides with the borders of modern-day Odisha. The modern state of Orissa was established on 1 April 1936, as a province in British India, and consisted predominantly of Odia-speaking regions. April 1 is celebrated as Odisha Day (Utkala Dibasa) . The region is also known as Utkala and is mentioned in India's national anthem, "Jana Gana Mana". Cuttack was made the capital of the region by Anantavarman Chodaganga in c. 1135, after which the city was used as the capital by many rulers, through the British era until 1948. Thereafter, Bhubaneswar became the capital of Odisha.

The Odisha state has a unicameral legislature. The Odisha Legislative Assembly consists of 147 elected members, and special office bearers such as the Speaker and Deputy Speaker, who are elected by the members. Assembly meetings are presided over by the Speaker, or by the Deputy Speaker in the Speaker's absence. Executive authority is vested in the Council of Ministers headed by the Chief Minister, although the titular head of government is the Governor of Odisha. The Governor is appointed by the President of India. The leader of the party or coalition with a majority in the Legislative Assembly is appointed as the Chief Minister by the Governor, and the Council of Ministers are appointed by the Governor on the advice of the Chief Minister. The Council of Ministers reports to the Legislative Assembly. The 147 elected representatives are called Members of the Legislative Assembly, or MLAs. One MLA may be nominated from the Anglo-Indian community by the Governor. The term of the office is for 5 years, unless the Assembly is dissolved prior to the completion of the term.

The Odisha Legislative Assembly is the unicameral state legislature of Odisha state in eastern India. The seat of the Legislative Assembly is at Bhubaneshwar, the capital of the state. The Legislative Assembly comprises 147 Members of Legislative Assembly.

This is a reference book. All the matter is just compiled and edited in nature, taken from the various sources which are in public domain.

This book will, undoubtedly, deepen our understanding of the economic prosperity and deterioration of Orissa in her past. It is hoped that every one interested in the economic history of Orissa will find this work quite informative and illuminative.

—*Editor*

ABOUT THE BOOK

Odisha is one of the 29 states of India. Located in eastern India, it is surrounded by the states of West Bengal to the north-east, Jharkhand to the north, Chhattisgarh to the west and north-west, and Andhra Pradesh to the south. Odisha has 485 kilometres (301 mi) of coastline along the Bay of Bengal on its east, from Balasore to Ganjam. It is the 9th largest state by area, and the 11th largest by population. It is also the 3rd most populous state of India in terms of tribal population. Odia (formerly known as Oriya) is the official and most widely spoken language, spoken by 33.2 million according to the 2001 Census. The main parties active in the politics of Odisha are the Biju Janata Dal, the Indian National Congress and Bhartiya Janata Party. Following the Odisha State Assembly Election in 2014, the Naveen Patnaik-led Biju Janata Dal stayed in power for the fourth consecutive term. The Government of Odisha and its 30 districts consists of an executive, led by the Governor of Odisha, a judiciary, and a legislative branch. Like other states in India, the head of state of Odisha is the Governor, appointed by the President of India on the advice of the Central government. His or her post is largely ceremonial. This book will, undoubtedly, deepen our understanding of the economic prosperity and deterioration of Orissa in her past. It is hoped that every one interested in the economic history of Orissa will find this work quite informative and illuminative.

Contents

1

State at a Glance

Odisha is one of the 29 states of India. Located in eastern India, it is surrounded by the states of West Bengal to the north-east, Jharkhand to the north, Chhattisgarh to the west and north-west, and Andhra Pradesh to the south.

Odisha has 485 kilometres (301 mi) of coastline along the Bay of Bengal on its east, from Balasore to Ganjam. It is the 9th largest state by area, and the 11th largest by population. It is also the 3rd most populous state of India in terms of tribal population. Odia (formerly known as *Oriya*) is the official and most widely spoken language, spoken by 33.2 million according to the 2001 Census.

The ancient kingdom of Kalinga, which was invaded by the Mauryan emperor Ashoka in 261 BCE resulting in the Kalinga War, coincides with the borders of modern-day Odisha. The modern state of Orissa was established on 1 April 1936, as a province in British India, and consisted predominantly of Odia-speaking regions. April 1 is celebrated as Odisha Day (Utkala Dibasa) . The region is also known as Utkala and is mentioned in India's national anthem, "Jana Gana Mana". Cuttack was made the capital of the region by Anantavarman Chodaganga in c. 1135, after which the city was used as the capital by many rulers, through the British era until 1948. Thereafter, Bhubaneswar became the capital of Odisha.

ETYMOLOGY

The term "Odisha" is derived from the ancient Prakrit word *"Odda Visaya"* (also *"Udra Bibhasha"* or *"Odra Bibhasha"*) as in the Tirumalai inscription of Rajendra Chola I, which is dated to 1025.

Sarala Das, who translated the *Mahabharata* into the Odia language in the 15th century, calls the region *Odra Rashtra* and *Odisha*. The inscriptions of Kapilendra Deva of the Gajapati Kingdom (1435–67) on the walls of temples in Puri call the region *Odisha* or *Odisha Rajya*.

The name of the state was changed from Orissa to Odisha, and the name of its language from Oriya to Odia, in 2011, by the passage of the *Orissa (Alteration of Name) Bill, 2010* and the *Constitution (113th Amendment) Bill, 2010* in the Parliament. After a brief debate, the lower house, Lok Sabha, passed the bill and amendment on 9 November 2010. On 24 March 2011, Rajya Sabha, the upper house of Parliament, also passed the bill and the amendment.

CULTURE

Cuisine

Odisha has a culinary tradition spanning centuries. The kitchen of the Shri Jagannath Temple, Puri is reputed to be the largest in the world, with 1,000 chefs, working around 752 wood-burning clay hearths called *chulas*, to feed over 10,000 people each day.

The syrupy dessert Pahala rasgulla made in Odisha is known throughout the world. Chhenapoda is another major Odisha sweet cuisine, which originated in Nayagarh.

Except these Pakhala is considered as traditional food of every Odia family . Chhena jhilipi of Nimapada, Mudhi mansa of Baripada, Aloodum dahibara of Cuttack, various pancakes prepared during festivals are some important cuisine of the state. With this Santula and dalmaa are some of the cuisine of the state .

Dance

Odissi (Orissi) dance and music are classical art forms. Odissi is the oldest surviving dance form in India on the basis of archaeological evidence. Odissi has a long, unbroken tradition of 2,000 years, and finds mention in the *Natyashastra* of Bharatamuni, possibly written c. 200 BC.

However, the dance form nearly became extinct during the British period, only to be revived after India's independence by a few gurus.

The variety of dances includes Ghumura Dance, Chhau dance, Jhumair, Mahari dance, and Gotipua.

Tourism

The Lingaraja Temple at Bhubaneswar has a 150-foot (46 m) high deula while the Jagannath Temple, Puri is about 200 feet (61 m) high and dominates the skyline. Only a portion of the Konark Sun Temple, the largest of the temples of the "Holy Golden Triangle" exists today, and it is still staggering in size. It stands out as a masterpiece in Odisha architecture. Sarala

Temple, regarded as one of the most spiritually elevated expressions of Shaktism is in Jagatsinghpur district. It is also one of the holiest places in Odisha & a major tourist attraction. Maa tarini temple situated in Kendujhar district is also a famous pilgrimage destination. Every day thousands of coconuts are given to Maa Tarini by devotees for fulfilling their wishes.

The Rath Yatra in Jagannath Temple, Puri

Odisha's varying topography – from the wooded Eastern Ghats to the fertile river basin – has proven ideal for evolution of compact and unique ecosystems. This creates treasure troves of flora and fauna that are inviting to many migratory species of birds and reptiles. Bhitarkanika National Park is famous for its second largest mangrove ecosystem. The bird sanctuary in Chilika Lake (Asia's largest brackish water lake) and the tiger reserve and waterfalls in Simlipal National Park are integral parts eco-tourism in Odisha, arranged by Odisha Tourism. Daringbadi, known as "Kashmir of Odisha," is a hill station in the Kandhamal district of Odisha. Chandipur, a calm and serene site, is mostly unexplored by tourists. The unique specialty of this beach is the ebb tides that recede up to 4 km and tend to disappear rhythmically.

The share of foreign tourists' arrival in the State is below one percent of total foreign tourist arrivals at all India level.

HISTORY OF ODISHA

The name Odisha refers to the current state in India. In different eras the region and parts of the region were known by different names. The boundaries of the region also have varied over the ages.

Lingaraja Temple built by the Somavanshi king Jajati Keshari

Human history in Odisha begins in the Lower Paleolithic era, as Acheulian tools dating to the period have been discovered in various places in the region. The early history of Odisha can be traced back to the mentions found in ancient texts like the *Mahabharata, Maha Govinda Sutta* and some *Puranas*. In 261 BCE, Ashoka of the Mauryan dynasty conquered the region in the bloody Kalinga Warwhich was fought at the banks of River Daya near present-day Bhubaneswar. The resulting bloodshed and suffering of the war deeply affected Ashoka. He turned into a pacifist and converted to Buddhism. He sent peace emissaries to various neighbouring nations. Thus as an indirect consequence, the event caused the spread of Buddhism in Asia.

The region was also known to other kingdoms in region of East Indies due to maritime trade relations.

The year 1568 CE is considered a pivotal point in the region's history. In 1568 CE, the region was conquered by the armies of the Sultanate of Bengal led by the iconoclast general Kalapahad. The region lost its political identity. The following rulers of the region were more tributary lords than actual kings. After 1751, the Marathas gained control of the region for almost half a decade. In 1803, the region was passed onto the British empire. The British divided the region into parts of other provinces. In 1936, the province of Odisha was formed on the basis of populations of Odia-speaking people.

Prehistoric Acheulian tools dating to Lower Paleolithic era have been discovered in various places in the region, implying an early settlement by humans. Kalinga has been mentioned in ancient texts like *Mahabharata*, *Vayu Purana* and *Mahagovinda Suttanta*. The Sabar people of Odisha have also been mentioned in the Mahabharata. Baudhayana mentions Kalinga as not yet being influenced by Vedic traditions, implying it followed mostly tribal traditions.

Hathigumpha on the Udayagiri Hills built in c. 150 BCE

Shanti Stupa at Dhauli is the location where Kalinga War was fought in c. 260 BCE

Ashoka of the Mauryan dynasty conquered Kalinga in the bloody Kalinga War in 261 BCE,which was the eighth year of his reign. According to his own edicts, in that war about 100,000 people were killed, 150,000 were captured and more were affected. The resulting bloodshed and suffering of the war is said to have deeply affected Ashoka. He turned into a pacifist and converted to Buddhism.

By c. 150 CE, emperor Kharavela, who was possibly a contemporary of Demetrius I of Bactria, conquered a major part of the Indian sub-continent. Kharavela was a Jain ruler. He also built the monastery atop the Udayagiri hill. Subsequently, the region was ruled by monarchs, such as Samudragupta and Shashanka. It was also a part of Harsha's empire.

Later, the kings of the Somavamsi dynasty began to unite the region. By the reign of Yayati II, c. 1025 CE, they had integrated the region into a single kingdom. Yayati II is supposed to have built the Lingaraj temple at Bhubaneswar. They were replaced by the Eastern Ganga dynasty. Notable rulers of the dynasty were Anantavarman Chodaganga, who began re-construction on the present-day Shri Jagannath Temple in Puri (c. 1135), and Narasimhadeva I, who constructed the Konark temple (c. 1250).

The Eastern Ganga Dynasty was followed by the Gajapati Kingdom. The region resisted integration into the Mughal empire until 1568, when it was conquered by Sultanate of Bengal. Mukunda Deva, who is considered the last independent king of Kalinga, was defeated and was killed in battle by a rebel Ramachandra Bhanja. Ramachandra Bhanja himself was killed by Bayazid Khan Karrani. In 1591, Man Singh I, then governor of Bihar, led an army to take Odisha from the Karranis of Bengal. They agreed to treaty because their leader Qutlu Khan Lohani had recently died. But, they then broke the treaty by attacking the temple town of Puri. Man Singh returned in 1592 and pacified the region.

Orissa was the first subah (imperial top-level province) added to Akbar's fifteen by Shah Jahan. It had Cuttack as seat and bordered Bihar, Bengal and Golconda subahs as well as the remaining independent and tributary chiefs. From 1717, the Orissa and Bihar governors were reduced to deputies of the Nawab (later Nizam) of the pseudo-autonomous Bengal Subah.

In 1751, the Nawab of Bengal Alivardi Khan ceded the region to the Maratha Empire.

The British had occupied the Northern Circars, comprising the southern coast of Odisha, as a result of the 2nd Carnatic War by 1760, and incorporated them into the Madras Presidency gradually. In 1803, the British ousted the Marathas from the Puri-Cuttack region of Odisha during the Second Anglo-Maratha War. The northern and western districts of Odisha were incorporated into the Bengal Presidency.

The Orissa famine of 1866 caused an estimated 1 million deaths. Following this, large-scale irrigation projects were undertaken. In 1903, the Utkal Sammilani organisation was founded to demand the unification of Odia-speaking regions into one state. On 1 April 1912, the Bihar and Orissa Province was formed. On 1 April 1936, Bihar and Orissa were split into separate provinces. The new province of Orissa came into existence on a linguistic basis during the British rule in India, with Sir John Austen Hubback as the first governor. Following India's independence, on 15 August 1947, 27 princely states signed the document to join Orissa.

Historical names of Odisha

The region which comprises the modern-day Odisha was not known by the same name throughout history. It and parts of it were referred by different names in different era.

- *Kalinga*: According to some scriptures (Mahabharata and some Puranas), a king Bali, the Vairocana, the son of Sutapa, had no sons. So, he requested the sage, Dirghatamas, to bless him with sons. The sage is said to have begotten five sons through his wife, the queen Sudesna. The princes were named Anga, Vanga, Kalinga, Sumha and Pundra.The princes later founded kingdoms named after themselves. The prince Vanga founded Vanga kingdom, in the current day region of Bangladesh and part of West Bengal. The prince Kalinga founded the kingdom of Kalinga, in the current day region of coastal Odisha, including the Northern Circars. Ptolemy, Pliny the elder and Claudius Aelianus have also mentioned one Calinga in their texts.

- *Utkala*: Utkala was a part of Kalinga in some parts of Mahabharata. Karna is mentioned to have conquered kingdom of Utkala among others. But, according to other texts like Raghuvasma and Brahma Purana, they were separate kingdoms. There are several views regarding the etymology of the name. Utkala may have meant northern (*uttara*) part of Kalinga or *ut-Kalinga*. *Utkala desha* (country or land) may have meant the land of "finest art" (*utkarsha kala*). There are also other arguments regarding the origin of the name.

- *Mahakantara*: This name has been found in some Gupta-era inscriptions. It literally means "great forest" and it is usually identified with the modern-day Kalahandiand Jeypore region. The Mahabharata also mentions a Kantara, which may have or may not have referred to the same region.

- *Udra*: Udra (also *Urda-desha*) may have originally referred to an ethnic group or tribe called Udra. But later may have referred to the kingdom of Udra, around the coastal region of Odisha.

- *Orda*: Odra (also *Orda-desha*) similar to Udra, may have meant a tribe of people called Odra, but later came to refer to the land of Odras.

- *Oddiyana*: Oddiyana, mentioned in some Buddhist texts, according to some scholars may have referred to Odisha.

- *Kamala Mandala*: Literally "lotus region", a c. 13th-century inscription found in Narla in Kalahandi refers to the region by this name.

- *South Kosala*: South Kosala (also *Dakshina Kosala*) may refer to the modern-day Chhattisgarh and some part of Western Odisha. It should not be confused with Kosala, which is in current day Uttar Pradesh. According to Ramayana, one of Rama's sons Lava ruled *Uttara Kosala* and his other son Kusha ruled over this region.

- *Kongoda*: A copper plate found in Ganjam district refers to region as Kongoda (also spelled Kangoda).

- *Trikalinga*: This name has been found inscribed on some copper plates found in Sonepur. Tri-Kalinga may have literally meant "three Kalingas" and may have referred to the three states of Kalinga, South Kosala and Kangoda.

- *Chedi*: Chedi (also known as *Chedirashtra*) referred to the kingdom of Kharavela. It was named after his dynasty, Chedi (also *Cheti* dynasty and Mahameghavahana dynasty). It should not be confused with Chedi kingdom of western India.

- *Tosali*: Tosali (also spelled *Toshali*) referred to a city and the region around it was called *Tosala*, possibly a subdivision of Kalinga in Ashoka-era. The capital of Tosala has been placed in modern-day Dhauli. In later era (c. 600 CE), North Tosali (*Uttara Tosali*) and South Tosali (*Daskhina Tosali*) have been mentioned, which were possibly kingdoms north and south of the Mahanadi river.
- *Uranshin*: The name has been used by some 10th century Arab geographers.
- *Jajnagar*: The name used for Odisha in the Tabaqat-i-Nasiri (c. 1260), Tarikh-i-Firuz Shahi (c. 1357), and other texts of the period.
- *Odivissa*: A name used in some Buddhist texts, including in those by Taranatha.

Prehistory

140 million years ago (mya), the peninsular India, including Odisha, was a part of the Gondwana supercontinent. Due to this, some of the oldest rocks in the subcontinent, dating to Precambrian times, are found in Odisha. Some of the rocks, like the Mayurbhanj granite pluton, have been dated to 3.09 billion years ago (Ga). The coal-fields in Mahanadiand Ib river basins are known to be one of the richest sites for fossils in the subcontinent. This has led to the discovery of new species, like the charophytes from the PermianPeriod, which were found in the Talcher region and the Upper Permian megaspores from the Ib river area.

In the districts of Mayurbhanj, Keonjhar, Sundargarh and Sambalpur, Acheulian tools dating to Lower Paleolithic times have been discovered. The Gudahandi hills in Kalahandi district have rock carvings and paintings dating to Upper Paleolithic. From Kuchai, near Baripada, various Neolithic tools like hoes, chisels, pounders, mace heads, grinding stones and also pieces of pottery. Prehistoric paintings and inscriptions have also been found in Garjan Dongar in Sundergarh district, and Ushakothi in Sambalpur district and Vimkramkhol in

Jharsuguda district. There has been an uncertainty about the inscriptions at Ushakothi and Vimkramkhol regarding whether they are in a proto-Brahmi script. Yogimath near Khariar has cave paintings from the Neolithic.

Ancient Odisha

Ancient Texts

According to some scriptures (Mahabharata and some Puranas), a king Bali, the Vairocana and the son of Sutapa, had no sons. So, he requested the sage, Dirghatamas, to bless him with sons. The sage is said to have begotten five sons through his wife, the queen Sudesna. The princes were named Anga, Vanga, Kalinga, Sumha and Pundra. The princes later founded kingdoms named after themselves. The prince Vanga founded Vanga kingdom, in the current day region of Bangladesh and part of West Bengal. The prince Kalinga founded the kingdom of Kalinga, in the current day region of coastal Odisha, including the North Sircars.

The Mahabharata also mentions Kalinga several more times. Srutayudha, the king of Kalinga, son of Varuna and river Parnasa, had joined the Kaurava camp in the Kurukshetra War. He had been given a divine mace by his father on request of his mother, which protected him as long he wielded it. But, Varuna had warned his son, that using it on a non-combatant will cause the death of the wielder himself. In the frenzy of battle, harried by Arjuna's arrows, he made the mistake of launching it at Krishna, Arjuna's charioteer, who was unarmed. The mace bounced off Krishna and killed Srutayudha. The archer who killed Krishna, Jara Savara, and Ekalavya are said to have belonged to the Sabar people of Odisha.

In the Buddhist text, Mahagovinda Suttanta, Kalinga and its ruler, Sattabhu, have been mentioned.

In the 6th century *sutrakara* (chronicler), Baudhayana, mentions Kalinga as not yet being influenced by Vedic traditions. He also warns his people from visiting Kalinga (among other kingdoms), saying one who visits it must perform penance.

Pre-Mauryan

Mahapadma Nanda the ruler of Magadha is presumed to have conquered Kalinga during his reign around c. 350 BCE. The Hathigumpha inscriptions mentions the suzerainty of the Nandas in the Kalinga region. The inscriptions also mention irrigation projects undertaken by the Nanda kings in the state during their reign.

In Asurgarh, beads and punched coins belonging to an unknown king dating to the pre-Mauryan period have been discovered.

Mauryan occupation

Ashoka of the Mauryan dynasty conquered Kalinga in the bloody Kalinga War in 261 BCE which was the 8th year of his reign. According to his own edicts, the war about 1,000,000 people were killed, 1,500,000 were captured and several more were affected. The resulting bloodshed and suffering of the war deeply affected Ashoka. He turned into a pacifist and converted to Buddhism.

The Kalingans had used personnel from the *Atavika* region, which was in the west of Kalinga, during the war. According to his edicts, Ashoka conquered the coastal region of Kalinga but didn't try to conquer the *Atavika* region. The Mauryans governed the Kalinga region as a province. They used Tosali as the regional capital and judiciary center. A *humara* (viceroy) ruled from Tosali, modern-day Dhauli. *Samapa*, modern-day Jaugada, was another administrative centre. Ashoka erected two edicts in the region, at Jaugada and Dhauli.

Kharavela

In the 1st century BCE, Mahameghavana established the Mahameghavahana dynasty in Kalinga. Kharavela was the third ruler of the dynasty. He reigned in the second half of the 1st century BCE. Most of the information about Kharavela comes from the Hathigumpha inscription in Udayagiri near Bhubaneswar. The inscription also calls the dynasty as Chedi (also spelled Cheti) but it is not the same as the Chedi kingdom of western India. The inscription records his life from his boyhood to his 13th regnal year.

- *Reigning year 1–5* : Kharavela took up the administration after the premature death of his father as a yuvaraj (heir apparent). He ascended to the throne as a proper King when he came of age at 24, around c. 170 BCE, but the date is contentious by several decades. In the first year of his coronation, he repaired the gates and ramparts of his capital *Kalinganagari* which had been damaged by storm. In the second year, he invaded the territory of the Satavahana king Satakarni I and marching up to the *Kanha-bemna* river (possibly Krishna river) stormed the city of Musikas. In the 3rd year of his reign, he organized various performances of dance and music and delighted the people of the capital. In the fourth year, he again invaded the Satavahana kingdom and extended his political supremacy over the region. In the fifth year he is known to have renovated the aqueduct that was originally excavated three hundred years back by the Nandas.

- *Reigning year 6–10* : In the sixth year, he remitted taxes and gave benevolences both in urban and rural areas of his kingdom. The account of his seventh year is not known. But that year his chief queen, Queen of *Vajiraghara* ("The Queen of the Diamond Palace") gave birth to a child. In his eighth regnal year he led a military expedition against *Rajagaha* (Rajagriha). By that time the Yavana (Indo-Greeks) who were in possession of Mathura were advancing towards Pataliputra. But getting the news of the triumph of Kharavela at Rajagriha the Yavana king had to retreat to Mathura. Kharavela pursued the Yavana ruler, *Dimita* (possibly Demetrius I) and purged them out of Mathura, which was an important seat of Jain religion and culture. In commemoration of this achievement, he built a victory palace in Kalinga at a cost of thirty-eight hundred thousand *penas* during the ninth year of his reign. In the tenth regnal year, he again invaded northern India the account of which is not clearly known.

- *Reigning year 11–13* : In the eleventh year of his reign, Kharavela defeated the Dramira country which had been in existence for hundred and thirteen years before his time. In the twelfth year, he invaded northern India for the third time and advanced as far as Uttarapatha. On his return, he terrorized Magadha. Bahasatimita (a Shunga king), the king of Magadha surrendered and Kharavela brought back the statue of *Kalinga Jina*. Kalinga Jina was the statue of Rishabhanatha, which had been taken away from Kalinga by Mahapadmananda three hundred years back and its restoration was considered to be a great achievement of Kharavela. In his thirteenth reigning year, Kharavela excavated a number of cave-dwellings in the Kumari hills for the Jain monks and bestowed endowments for them. Jainism greatly flourished in Kalinga under the patronage of Kharavela. He was also extending liberal patronage towards other religious communities and earned great reputation as the worshipper of all faiths and the repairers of all temples. He also built the caves at Udayagiri and Khandagiri for Jain monks.

The record stops at his 13th regnal year. It is presumed that he was succeeded by his son, Kudepasiri. The Mahameghavahana dynasty (or a successor *Sada* dynasty) probably continued to rule over Kalinga and Mahishaka as evident from the inscriptions and coins discovered at Guntupalli and Velpuru, Andhra Pradesh, which mention a series of rulers with the suffix *Sada*.

Kushanas, Satavahanas and Murundas

Odisha Timeline

500 BCE – 1200 CE:

c. 350 BCE Mahapadma Nanda conquers Kalinga

261 BCE   Ashoka conquers Kalinga in the Kalinga War

c. 170 BCE Coronation of Kharavela

600 CE   Shashanka invades Kalinga

c. 639 CE   Hiuen-Tsang visits Oddiyana

c. 885 CE   Janmejaya I establishes the Somavamsi dynasty

c. 1135 CE   Anantavarman Chodaganga shifts his capital to Kataka

c. 1245 CE   Narasimhadeva I builds the Konark temple

c. 1278 CE   Queen Chadrika builds the Ananta Vasudeva Temple

Gautamiputra Satkarni of Satavahana dynasty possibly held some sway over some parts Kalinga.

The Kushana empire may have reached Kalinga or parts of it during the first three centuries of the common era as evident from coins found at several places in notably in Jaugada, Sisupalgarh and Gurubai in Manikapatana (Puri) among others. It should be noted that more imitation coins are found than real ones. So, the local rulers possibly circulated them in the post-Kushana period. There is coin of one Maharaja Rajadhiraja Dharmadamadhara which has been found in Sisupalgarh. There is a Kushana motif on one side and a human head on the other.

During the 3rd century, a tribe called Murundas, ruled from Pataliputra. They have been speculated to have arrived from Central Asia. They used to issue coins similar to Kushana coins.

But other than these mostly numismatic evidences, this period of history is mostly in the dark.

Guptas, Matharas and Sharabhapuriyas

In c. 313 BCE, a princess of Kalinga, Hemamala, is recorded to have fled the kingdom with a tooth of Buddha, a sacred relic, hidden in her hair and presented it to king Sirimeghavanna of Sri Lanka. According to the legend, Khema took a tooth from the pyre of Buddha and later gave in to a king, Brahmadutta. He built a temple at a city called Dantapura. After several generations, during the reign the Guhasiva, the prince of Ujjain came to Dantapura to worhship the relic. He married the daughter of Guhasiva, Hemamala, and was later called Dantakumara (Prince Tooth). When a king attacked Kalinga, Dantakumara and Hemamala fled with the relic to protect it. Samudragupta (reign c. 335 – c. 375 CE) is presumed to have conquered the region, as in his Allahabad inscription, it has been mentioned that, he had conquered Mahêndra of Kôsala, Vyâghraraja of Mahâkantâra, Mantarâja of Kêrala, Mahêndra of Pishtapura, Svâmidatta of Kottûra on the hill, Damana of Êrandapalla, Vishnugôpa of Kâñchi, Nîlarâija of Avamukta, Hastivarman of Vengî, Ugrasêna of Palakka, Kubêra of Dêvarâshtra, Dhanamjaya of Kusthalapura, and others. Pishtapura (modern-day Pithapuram) is presumed to be the then capital of Kalinga. Mahakantara is presumed to be parts of western Odisha and Central India. Kottura is traced to modern day Ganjam district.

In post-Samudragupta period, a new dynasty called Matharas arose in south Kalinga, they ruled from Pishtapura but also issued copper grants from Simhapura. Their kingdom was probably spread from Mahanadi to Godavari. Another dynasty of rulers arose in western Odisha during post-Gupta period, they are called Sharabhapuriya dynasty. Not much is known about this dynasty. Everything known about them, comes from the inscriptions on copper plates and coins. They may or may not have also been known as the Amararyakula dynasty. This dynasty is supposed to have started by one Sarabha, who may have been a feudal chief under the Guptas. They ruled over the modern-day region of Raipur, Bilaspur and Kalahandi. Their rule lasted from c. 499 to about 700 CE.

Eastern Ganga Dynasty

Indravarman I is assumed to be the earliest known king of the Eastern Ganga dynasty. His Jirjingi grant mentions no predecessors and was issued in his 39th regnal year, c. 537 CE. He had his capital at Dantapura. Another plate found also mentions him defeating a Vishnukundina king called Indra Bhattaraka. Many rulers of this dynasty went by the title *Trikalingadhipati*, literally the "lord of the three Kalingas". The capital was later shifted to Kalinganagara, later during the reign of Devendravarman I (c. 652–682?).

The Jagannath temple was built by rulers of the Eastern Ganga dynasty.

Narasimhadeva I is known to have built the Konark temple.

During this period, c. 639 CE, Xuanzang visited this region, he notes that Buddhism was widely practiced in this region. He mentions the existence of the monastery called Puphagiri. The sites were lost until recently. New excavations have found several Buddhist monuments dating to this period. Odisha was conquered by Rajendra Chola I of the Chola dynasty in the early 11th century.

The capital was again shifted to Kataka by Anantavarman Chodaganga in 1135. He is said to have started building the Puri Jagannath temple. The temple was later completed by his successor Anangabhima Deva III. Narasimha Deva I is known to have built the Konark temple.

In 1187, Nissanka Malla who ascended to the throne in Sri Lanka claimed to have descended from Kalinga. He may have born in 1157 in the capital of Kalinga, Sinhapura (modern day Srikakulam, now in Andhra Pradesh). In 1215, an invader from Kalinga, called Kalinga Magha landed in Sri Lanka and had an oppressive reign of 21 years.

By the early 12th century, Kalinga had been conquered by Kulothunga Chola I and his general Karunakara Tondaiman. The literary work called Kalingathu Parani, is written in praise of the invasion.

According to the text Tabaqat-i-Nasiri, the ruler of Jajnagar (Kalinga) began to harass the Lukhnauti (Bengal) ruler in 1243. Tughral Tughan Khan the governor of Bengal advanced against Jajnagar in March 1244. They armies encountered after a month at the frontier fort of Katashin and the Kalingan army retreated after taking losses. Later, when the army of Khan was having lunch, the Kalingan army flanked them and attacked. The defeated army of Khan then retreated.

Medieval Odisha

Odisha Timeline

1200 CE - 1800 CE:

1434 CE	Coronation of Kapilendradeva
c. 1467 CE	Sarala Dasa writes the Odia Mahabharata

1559 CE	Mukunda Deva seizes the throne
1568 CE	Kalapahad invades Odisha
3 March 1575	Battle of Tukaroi takes place in Balasore
1623	Shah Jahan visits Odisha
1751	Alivardi Khan cedes Odisha to Marathas

Gajapati Dynasty

The Gajapati Dynasty was established by Kapilendra Deva in 1435, after the fall of the last Eastern Ganga king, Bhanudeva IV. The dynasty is also known as a Suryavamsi dynasty. In about 1450, Kapilendra Deva installed his eldest son, Hamira, as the governor of Rajamundry and Kondavidu. Kapilendra Deva managed spread his kingdom from Ganga in the north to as far as Bidar in the south by 1457.

During Kapilendra Deva's reign, Sarala Dasa, the Odia poet, wrote the Odia Mahabharata and his other works.

When Kapilendra Deva died in 1467, a civil war occurred to capture the throne, among his sons. In the end, Purushottama Devasucceeded in securing the throne in 1484 by defeating Hamvira.

But, during this period significant southern parts of the empire were lost to Saluva Narasimha, the ruler of Vijayanagara. By the time of his death, he had managed to recover some these territories.

He was succeeded by his son, Prataparudra Deva, in 1497. Immediately, he had to face the armies of Alauddin Husain Shah of Bengal. During his reign, Alauddin Husain Shah attacked again in 1508, this time the Muslim army marched up to Puri. In 1512 Krishna Deva Raya of the Vijayanagara Empireinvaded Kalinga and defeated the forces of the Gajapati Kingdom. In 1522, Quli Qutb Shah of Golconda ousted the Odia army from Krishna-Godavari tract.

Govinda Vidyadhara was a minister under, Gajapati king, Prataparudra Deva. But, he rebelled against him and succeeded in ascending the throne in 1541, after murdering the two sons of Prataparudra Deva.

Bhoi Dynasty

The Bhoi Dynasty was founded by Govinda Vidyadhara who came to throne in a bloody coup, in 1541. The dynasty was short-lived and during this period the kingdom came under conflict with neighbouring kingdoms and reeled with civil wars. First, Raghubhanja Chhotray who was the nephew of Govinda Vidyadhara, became a rebel.

Govinda was succeeded by his son, Chakrapratap, who was an unpopular ruler. After he died in 1557, a minister called Mukunda Deva rebelled. He killed the last two Bhoi kings and squashed the rebellion of Raghubhanja Chhotray. After that, he declared himself the ruler of Odisha.

Mukunda Deva

Mukunda Deva (also known as Mukunda Harichandana) came to throne, in 1559, in a bloody coup. According to the *Madala Panji* (temple records), he was a Chalukya. During this period, Odisha was going through many internal conflicts. Mukunda stuck an alliance with Akbar, that he made him a foe of Sulaiman Khan Karrani, the ruler of Bengal. Sulaiman sent his son, Bayazid Khan Karrani and his infamous general, Kalapahad, to conquer Odisha, in 1567.

Mukunda met the forces in the north but had to withdraw to stop a rebellion after signing a treaty with the Sultan's son. Mukunda was killed in a battle with the rebel forces led by Ramachandra Bhanja. Ramachandra Bhanja was a feudal lord under Mukunda, who had rebelled. He himself got caught up in the conflict and was murdered by Bayazid. Akbar was preparing for the invasion of Chittor, so he was unable to respond. Kalapahad ran across the kingdom in a plundering spree and destroyed several temples. By end of 1568, Odisha was under the control of Sulaiman Khan Karrani.

During this period, Ramachandra Deva I, who was the son of a general and had been imprisoned by Mukunda, escaped from prison and fled to Vizagapatam.

1568

1568 is considered an important date in the history of Odisha, as Mukunda Deva is considered the last independent ruler of Odisha. After 1568, the region saw a steady decline. Odisha was not to be an independent kingdom again.

Later in 1920, Odia playwright, Ashwini Kumar Ghose wrote a play called *Kala Pahada* based on the exploits of Kalapahad and the tragic death of Mukunda Deva. The play is considered one of the greatest tragedies in Odia literature.

Bengal (Karrani) rule

In 1568, Odisha came under the control of Sulaiman Khan Karrani of the Karrani dynasty, who was the ruler of Sultanate of Bengal.

In the Battle of Tukaroi, which took place in modern-day Balasore, Daud Khan Karrani was defeated and retreated deep into Odisha. The battle led to the Treaty of Katak in which Daud ceded the whole of Bengal and Bihar, retaining only Odisha. The treaty eventually failed after the death of Munim Khan (governor of Bengal and Bihar) who died at the age of 80. Daud took the opportunity and invaded Bengal. This led to the Battle of Rajmahal in 1576, where Daud was defeated and executed.

Mughal rule

In 1590, Qutlu Khan Lohani, an officer of Daud, declared himself independent and assumed the title of "Qutlu Shah". Raja Man Singh who was the Mughal governor of Bihar, started an expedition against him. Before facing Man Singh, Qutlu Shah died. Qutlu Khan's son Nasir Khan, after little resistance, accepted Mughal sovereignty and paid homage to Man Singh on 15 August 1590. Nasir Khan was then appointed Governor of Odisha and signed a treaty which ceded the region of Puri. Nasir Khan remained faithful to the Mughal empire for two years but after that he violated the conditions of his treaty by laying siege to the Jagannath Temple of Puri. Man Singh attacked Nasir Khan and decisively defeated him on 18 April

1592 in a battle near the present day Midnapore town. By 1593, Odisha had passed completely to the Mughal empire and was a part of Bengal Subah.

Under Akbar

Raja Ramachandra Deva, the king of Khurda, had accepted Akbar's suzerainty. Akbar mostly followed a policy of non-interference in the local chieftains' matters. After Akbar, his son, Jahangir came to power, who followed a different policy. Under him, Odisha was made into a separate Subah and a governor, titled *Subahdar*, ruled in the name of the Mughal emperor.

Under Jahangir

Quasim Khan was appointed the governor of Odisha in 1606. During this period, the king of Khurda, Purusottam Deva was attacked by Mughal armies led by Kesho Das. He was defeated, and had to offer his sister and daughter along with dowry to buy peace.

In 1611, Kalyan Mal, son of Todar Mal came to be the governor of Odisha. Kalyan Mal also attacked and defeated Purusottam Deva, who had to send his daughter to the Mughal harem. In 1617, Kalyan was recalled to the court.

In 1617, Mukarram Khan became the governor of Odisha. He also tried to attack Purusottam Deva. But, Purusottam Deva fled from Khurda. In 1621, Ahmad Beg was made the governor of Odisha. Purusottam Deva died in exile in 1622 and was succeed by his son Narasimha Deva. According to the Madala Panji (temple chronicles), prince Shah Jahan had visited Odisha in 1623, which was just after his rebellion. Ahmad Beg remained governor until 1628.

Under Shah Jahan

In 1628, Shah Jahan became the Mughal emperor and Muhammad Baqar Khan was appointed the governor of Odisha. He extended his influence well into the kingdom of Golconda. In 1632, he was recalled. Shah Shuja was appointed by Shah

Jahan as the Subahdar of Bengal from 1639 until 1660. From 1645 onwards, a deputy of Shuja called Zaman Teharani was the governor of Odisha.

Orissa was the first subah (imperial top-level province) added to Akbar's fifteen by Shah Jahan. It had Cuttack as seat and bordered Bihar, Bengal and Golconda subahs, as well as the remaining independent and tributary chiefs. In 1647, Narasimha Deva was beheaded by a Mughal general called Fateh Khan.

Under Aurangzeb

In 1658, Shah Jahan took ill and Dara Shikoh took on as the royal regent.

This led to a war of succession in which Aurangzeb emerged victorious in 1659. He imprisoned his own father, who later died in 1666. During this period of instability in the Mughal empire, several chieftains in Odisha had declared independence. Khan-i-Duran was appointed the governor under Aurangzeb and his reign was from 1660 to 1667. During this period, he crushed several rebel chieftains and subdued Mukunda Deva I, the then king of Khurda.

Under Murshid Quli Khan

In 1707, Aurangzeb died and the control of Mughals over Odisha began to weaken. Murshid Quli Khan was made governor of Odisha in 1714. In 1717, he was also made the Nawab of Bengal. He swore fealty to the Mughal emperor but he was an independent ruler for all purposes. He took several measures to increase revenues and create several new Jagirs. In 1727, on his death, his son-in-law, Shuja-ud-Din became the Nawab of Bengal. Before that he was a deputy of Murshid in Odisha. During his time, several tracts of land were lost to neighbouring kingdoms.

Under Shuja-ud-Din

In 1727, Taqi Khan, the son of Shuja-ud-Din, was made the governor. He got engaged in a war with Ramachandra Deva II.

Ramachandra Deva II was imprisoned and was converted to Islam. Ramachandra Deva II once visited Puri to see car festival. Taqi Khan was displeased by this advanced on Khurda and Ramachandra Deva II fled. Bhagirathi Kumar, son of Ramachandra Deva II, was declared king by Taqi Khan. Taqi Khan died in 1734. During his reign, several Islamic monuments were built in Odisha.

His successor, Murshid Quli Khan II (alias. Rustam Jung), a Naib Nazim (deputy governor) of Shuja-ud-Din and also his son-in-law, allowed worship in Puri and he is said to have given his daughter to Ramachandra Deva II in marriage.

He installed Padmanava Deva as king of Khurda in 1736 but replaced him by Birakesari Deva, son of Ramachandra Deva II in 1739.

Shuja-ud-Din died in 1739 and was replaced by his son, Sarfaraz Khan. Sarfaraz Khan was defeated and killed in the Battle of Giria by Alivardi Khan. Rustam Jung marched against Alivardi Khan but he was defeated. Alivardi Khan was not a popular ruler.

The Marathas started raiding Alivardi Khan's territory starting in 1742, aided by Rustam Jung and his allies. These raids used quick hit-and-run tactics and were called bargis. Alivardi Khan unable to check the raids ceded Odisha to Raghoji Bhonsle I in 1751.

During this period, the idols of Jaganatha and other deities were removed from the temple several times, and hidden to save them from iconoclasm.

Maratha rule

The river Subarnarekha served as the border between Bengal and Maratha-controlled Odisha. Marathas used to collect a pilgrimage tax at Puri, which was exempt for paupers.

In 1803, the British conquered the region during the Second Anglo-Maratha War, when most of the Maratha forces were engaged elsewhere.

Colonial era

Orissa Timeline

1800 CE - 1947 CE:

14 October 1803	Fort of Barabati falls to the British
1817	The Paika Rebellion
1866	The Great Famine of 1886 (*Na Anka Durvikhya*)
1 April 1936	Orissa became a separate province
15 August 1947	India becomes independent

1600-1803

The Portuguese were the first Europeans to build factories in Odisha. They had a settlement in Pipili in Balasore district. The British had established a settlement in Hariharpur (modern-day Jagatsinghpur), with the permission of the Mughal administrator, as early as 1633 to trade cotton goods. But it could not be maintain long because of the harsh climate, and Portuguese and Aracanese pirates.

Ruins of Barabati fort in Cuttack.

In 1765, Lord Clive acquired the *diwani* of Bengal, Bihar and Odisha from titular Mughal emperor, Shah Alam II. But, only the Midnapore district was meant by Odisha, as rest of it had passed on to the Marathas. Lord Clive had tried to negotiate the acquisition of Odisha from the Marathas. His successor, Warren Hastings, had also tried negotiating with the Marathas.

1803-1900

A Colonel Harcourt of the British Army sailed from Northern Circars on 3 August 1803 and landed on 25 August. He marched from Ganjamwith 5000 men on 8 September, to flush the Marathas out of the region. On 18 September, Harcourt took control of Puri. On 21 September, a second force had landed at Balasore and after taking control of the region, it sent reinforcements to Cuttack to help with the siege of the fort. On 14 October, the fort of Barbati was stormed and captured.

On 17 December 1803, Raghoji II Bhonsle of Nagpur signed the Treaty of Deogaon (also Deogarh) in Odisha with the British after the Battle of Laswari and gave up the province of Cuttack (which included *Mughalbandi*, the coastal part of Odisha, *Garhjat* the princely states of Western Odisha, Balasore port, and parts of Midnapore district of West Bengal).

Jaya Krushna Rajguru Mahapatra, known to the people as Jayee Rajguru, the royal preceptor to Mukunda Dev II (who was a minor) mobilised an army of Paika warriors and raised a revolt against the British in 1804. This is the first uprising against the British rule in Orissa. The Britishers, ultimately with the help of some treacherous natives ruthlessly suppressed the rebellion. Both Jayee Rajguru and the Raja were made prisoners. Later Jayee Rajguru was convicted and on 6 December 1806 hanged heinously by his legs tied to two different branches of Banyan tree and released to tear him to two parts at Midnapore. The Raja was released in 1807 since Jayee Rajguru had taken the entire responsibility of the uprising on him. Thus Jayee Rajguru is said to be the first martyr of the early freedom struggle against British rule. His sacrifice, however, did not go in vain. It laid the foundation of a major revolt 13 years after his Martyrdom.

In 1817, the British had to suppress the Paika rebellion. The Paika were a landed militia who were exempted from taxes in lieu of their services. They were dissatisfied with the new

British land laws and were led by Bakshi Jagabandhu, a commander of the king of Khurda.

Surendra Sai from Sambalpur region had started a rebellion against the British in 1827. During the Indian Rebellion of 1857, the princes of Odisha did not join the wars.

In 1866, Odisha was struck with a great famine, called *Na Anka Durvikhya* (literally *the nine number famine*) locally. The death toll has been estimated to be about one million spread across different regions. During the famine, Babu Bichitrananda Das and Gouri Shankar Roy decided to publish a magazine in Odia. The first issue of *Utakala Deepika*appeared on 4 August 1866 from the newly Cuttack Printing Press. It dealt with issue of famine. Though Christian missionaries had established a printing press in Cuttack in 1838, this was the first independent publication in Odia.

In 1870, Madhusudan Das became the first person from Odisha to acquire a graduate degree. He had completed his Bachelor of Arts from Calcutta University and later went on to acquire a Master of Arts from the same university in 1873. He also acquired a law degree in 1878. He went on to become one of the foremost leaders from the state.

After Madhusudan Das returned from Calcutta to Cuttack in 1881, the Utkal Sabha was formed in 1882. It marked the beginning of political activities in Odisha. In 1888, a durbarwas held in Cuttack during the visit of Lieutenant-Governor of Bengal, where the Utkal Sabha led by Gouri Shankar Roy presented the issue of bringing Odia-speaking territories under one administration.

1900-1947

In 1903, the Utkal Union Conference was founded. In 1911, Odisha and Bihar were separated from Bengal province to form a new single province. In 1912, the Orissa Tenancy Act was introduced the Bihar-Orissa Legislative Assembly. The previous Bengal Tenancy Act of 1885 was considered ill-suited for the conditions of the region. On 12 September 1913, the Orissa

Tenancy Act was passed, securing better rights and treatment for ryots in the region. In 1913, Sashibhusan Rath began publishing the first Odia daily newspaper, *Asha*, from Berhampur. Gopabandhu Das was the editor and wrote its editorials until 1919. In 1915, Gopabandhu Das began publishing a magazine called *Satyabadi*, to promote Odia literature and culture. On 4 October 1919, he started his own weekly newspaper, *Samaja*. In 1914, the revolutionary Bagha Jatin moved to a hideout in Kaptipada village in Mayurbhanj. On 9 September 1915, Bagha Jatin and his companions were discovered by the British and it resulted in a 75 minutes gunfight. On 10 September 1915, Bagha Jatin died of bullet wounds at the Balasore hospital.

In 1885, Indian National Congress was founded. In 1920, it adopted reorganization of provinces according to linguistic basis as one its agendas. This inspired many leaders in Odisha to form an Odisha Congress Committee and demand a separate province for the Odia-speaking population. In 1923, the Bhubanananda Odisha School Of Engineering was established in Cuttack. It was the first technical diploma institution in the region. In 1927, the districts of Cuttack and Balasore were hit by abnormal floods for the third successive year. About 28,756 families were affected by the floods according to the government report.

On 6 April 1930, a group of volunteers marched from Cuttack to Inchudi in Balasore. On 12 April, they defied the British salt tax law by making salt. On 1 April 1936, Odisha was granted the status of a separate province. Odisha Day (*Utkala Dibasa*) is celebrated locally every year on 1 April to mark the day. In 1936, Odisha has 6 districts: Cuttack, Puri, Balasore, Ganjam, Koraput, and Sambalpur. On 11 October 1938, Baji Rout, a ferry boy of 12 years, was shot dead by policemen in Dhenkanal district, when he refused to ferry them across the river. In 1943, the Utkal University was founded.

In March 1946, the foundation stone for the Hirakud Dam was laid by the Governor of Odisha, Sir Hawthrone Lewis. Also in 1946, the Central Rice Research Institute (CRRI) was established in Cuttack to prevent occurrences like the Bengal famine of 1943. On 22 July 1947, Biju Patnaik rescued the Indonesian Prime Minister Sutan Sjahrir and Vice President Mohammad Hatta from behind Dutch lines and flew them to Singapore in a Douglas C-47 Skytrain, disguised as crew members. They reached India on 24 July.

Post-independence

Orissa Timeline

1947 CE – Present:

1948	Capital of Odisha shifted from Cuttack to Bhubaneswar
1952	The first Kalinga Prize awarded
1953	Completion of the Hirakud Dam
1956	University College of Engineering, was established in Burla
1957	Odisha Sahitya Academy was established
12 February 1961	The building of Legislative Assembly of Odisha was inaugurated

1947-2000

On 27 May 1947, Harekrushna Mahatab took oath to form a Congress ministry. In 1946, it was decided that Bhubaneswar would replace Cuttack as the political capital of the state of Odisha. A year after India gained its independence from Britain, the task of designing had been granted to the German architect Otto Königsberger.

Also in 1948, construction on the Hirakud Dam began. By 1949, the 24 princely states had been integrated and Odisha had 13 districts: Cuttack, Puri, Balasore, Ganjam, Koraput, Sambalpur, Dhenkanal, Sundergarh, Keonjhar, Balangirpatna, Boudh-Kandhamal, Mayurbhanj and Kalahandi. On 12 May 1950, Mahatab resigned to join the Cabinet of India. Nabakrushna Choudhuri took over as the Chief Minister the same day.

In 1951, Biju Pattnaik made a donation to the UNESCO to establish the Kalinga Prize. It has been awarded every year since 1952 to people who have contributed to the popularization of science. On 12 February 1952, Nabakrushna Choudhuri took oath as the Chief Minister after the 1951 Assembly polls. In 1953, the 66 meters high and 25.4 km long Hirakud Dam was completed. In 1953, the Rourkela Steel Plant was planned to be built in collaboration with a West German consortium. On 19 October 1956, Nabakrushna Choudhuri resigned and Mahatab became the Chief Minister. In 1956, the first technical degree institution in the region, University College of Engineering, was established in Burla (presently it is known as Veer Surendra Sai University of Technology). In 1957, the Odisha Sahitya Academy was established to develop and promote Odia language and literature. On 13 January 1957, Prime Minister Jawaharlal Nehru officially inaugurated the Hirakud Dam. The 1957 Assembly polls were also won by the Congress party and on 6 April 1957 Harekrushna Mahatab took oath as the Chief Minister. On 22 May 1959, a coalition of Congress and Gantantra Parishad formed the government. On 21 February 1961, the coalition collapsed. On 25 February, President's rule was imposed on the state.

Legislative Assembly of Odishabuilding was inaugurated in 1961

On 12 February 1961, the new building of the Legislative Assembly of Odisha was inaugurated by Sarvepalli Radhakrishnan then Vice-President of India.

On 15 August 1961, the Regional Engineering College, Rourkela was founded. The mid-term polls were held in 1961 and Biju Pattnaik formed a ministry on 23 June 1961.

On 3 January 1962, the foundation stone of the Paradip Port was laid by Prime Minister Nehru. On 18 April 1966, it was declared the 8th major port of India.

Also in 1962, the Balimela Reservoir project was started. In August 1963, the Kamaraj Plan was formulated and Biju Patnaik was among the Chief Ministers to resign.

After him, Biren Mitra became the Chief Minister. In April 1964, a Hindustan Aeronautics Limited plant was set up in Sunabeda to manufacture Tumansky R-11 F2 engines for MIG-21 FLs.

In 1966, Mahatab left Indian National Congress to form a new party called the Jana Congress. After the 1967 Assembly polls, Rajendra Narayan Singh Deo became the Chief Minister of a coalition government consisting of the Swatantra Party and the Orissa Jana Congress.

In 1971 Assembly poll, the government was formed by a coalition of Utkal Congress, Swatantra Party and All India Jharkhand Party, with Biswanath Das as the Chief Minister. On 14 June 1972, Nandini Satpathy became the Chief Minister of Odisha, heading a Congress ministry.

On 1 March 1973, Chief Minister Nandini Satpathy resigned. In February 1974, mid-term polls were held. On 6 March 1974, Nandini Satpathy formed her second ministry.

On 19 December 1976, Nandini Satpathy resigned again. She was replaced by Binayak Acharya who remained in office for 4 months. In 1977, Nilamani Routray became the Chief Minister after the Assembly poll, and Janata Party remained in power until 1980. The 1980 Assembly poll resulted in Janaki Ballabh Patnaik, of Indian National Congress, as the Chief Minister.

In 1981, NALCO was founded with the collaboration of the Pechiney company of France. It was headquartered in Bhubaneswar. On 30 October 1984, Indira Gandhiwas in Bhubaneswar giving a speech. The next day she was assassinated.

In 1985, Janaki Ballabh Patnaik was re-elected as the Chief Minister. Sachidananda Routray, Odia poet and novelist, received the Jnanpith Award for his contributions to modern Odia poetry. On 22 May 1989, the Agni-I was tested fired at Chandipur. On 6 December 1989, Janaki Ballabh Patnaik resigned as the Chief Minister and on 7 December Hemananda Biswal was sworn in. On 16 December 1989, Rabi Ray becomes the Speaker of Lok Sabha and he held the position until 9 July 1991.

In 1990, Ranganath Misra became the 21st Chief Justice of India. In 1990, the Assembly polls were won by the Janata Dal and a government was formed under the leader of Biju Patnaik.

In 1992, four new districts were created, Gajapati, Malkangiri, Rayagada and Nabarangpur. In 1993, 10 more districts were created, Khurda, Nayagarh, Sonepur, Bargarh, Kendrapara, Jagatsinghpur, Jajpur, Nuapada, Angul and Bhadrak. In 1994, three more were craved out, Jharsuguda, Deogarh and Boudh.

This brought the number of districts in Odisha to 30. In 1993, Ranganath Misra became the first chairman of the National Human Rights Commission of India. The 1995 Assembly polls were won by the Indian National Congress and Janaki Ballabh Patnaik became the Chief Minister. On 22 January 1999, Australianmissionary Graham Staines and his two sons were murdered. Staineswas an Australian Christian missionary who, along with his two sons Philip (aged 10) and Timothy (aged 6), was burnt to death by a gang while sleeping in his station wagon at Manoharpur village in Keonjhar district in Odisha, India on 23 January 1999. In 2003, a Bajrang Dal activist, Dara Singh, was convicted of leading the gang that murdered Graham Staines and his sons, and was sentenced to life in prison. Soon afterwards,

Janaki Ballabh Patnaik resigned and was replaced by Giridhar Gamang. In October 1999, a cyclone struck Odisha causing economic loss estimated at \$2.5 billion (1999 USD) and about 10,000 deaths. In December 1999, Gamang also resigned. He was replaced by Hemananda Biswal on 7 December. In March 2000, Naveen Patnaik became the Chief Minister of a BJD-BJP alliance government.

2001-present

On 20 February 2014, the Odia language was given the status of a classical language of India, making it the sixth language to have the status.

2

Culture and Society

CULTURE OF ODISHA

Odisha (formerly Orissa) is one of the 29 states of India, located in the eastern coast. It is surrounded by the states of West Bengal to the north-east, Jharkhand to the north, Chhattisgarh to the west and north-west, Andhra Pradesh and Telangana to the south and south-west.

Odia (formerly known as *Oriya*) is the official and most widely spoken language, spoken by 33.2 million according to the 2001 Census. The modern state of Odisha was established on 1 April 1936, as a province in British India, and consisted predominantly of Odia-speaking regions. April 1 is celebrated as Odisha Day.

VISUAL ARTS

Other cultural attractions include the Jagannatha Temple in Puri, known for its annual Rath Yatra or Car Festival, the unique and beautiful appliqué artwork of Pipili, silver filigree ornamental works from Cuttack, *Pattachitra, tala chitra* (palm leaf engravings), famous stone utensils of Nilgiri (Balasore) and various tribal influenced cultures. The Sun Temple at Konark is famous for its architectural splendour while the *Sambalpuri textiles* equals it in its artistic grandeur.

Sand art

Sand sculpture is practised on the beaches at Puri. Fine-grained sand is mixed with water and shaped by the fingers. Odishan legend says that

"Poet Balarama Dasa, the author of Dandi Ramayana, was a great devotee of Lord Jagannath. Once during Ratha Yatra (Car Festival), he tried to climb the chariot of Lord Jagannath to offer his prayer. Since he wasn't allowed by the priests of the chariot to climb it and also insulted by them. With a great frustration and humiliation he came to the beach (Mahodadhi) and carved the statues of Lord Jagannath, Lord Balabhadra and Devi Subhadra on the Golden sand."

Religion

In its long history, Odisha has had a continuous tradition of dharmic religions especially Hinduism, Buddhism and Jainism. Ashoka's conquest of Kalinga (India) made Buddhism a principal religion in the state which led to establishment of numerous Stupas and buddhist learning centres. During Kharavela's reign Jainism found prominence. However, by middle of 9th century CE there was a revival of Hinduism as attested by numerous temples such as Mukteshwara, Lingaraja, Jagannath and Konark, which were erected starting from the late 7th century CE. Part of the revival in Hinduism was due to Adi Shankaracharya who proclaimed Puri to be one of the four holiest places or *Char Dham* for Hinduism. Odisha has therefore a syncretic mixture of the three dharmic religions as attested by the fact that the Jagannath Temple in Puri is considered to be holy by Hindus, Buddhists and Jains.

Presently, the majority of people in the state of Odisha are Hindus. As per the census of 2001, Odisha is the third largest Hindu populated state (as a percentage of population) in the country as illustrated in the 2001 census table and in this table. However, while Odisha is predominantly Hindu it is not monolithic. The state also has a Christian and Muslim minority. There is a rich cultural heritage in the state owing to Hindu faith. For example, Odisha is home to several Hindu saints. Sant Bhima Bhoi was a leader of the Mahima sect movement, Sarala Dasa, was the translator of the epic Mahabharata in Odia, Chaitanya Dasa was a Buddhistic-Vaishnava and writer of the *Nirguna Mahatmya*, Jayadeva was the author of the *Gita Govinda* and is recognized by the Sikhs as one of their most important bhagats. Swami Laxmananda Saraswati is a modern-day Hindu saint of Adivasi heritage.

Language

The official language of the state, spoken by the majority of the people is Odia. Odia belongs to the Indo-Aryan branch of the Indo-European language family, and is closely related to Bengali and Assamese. The tribal people or Adivasis of Odisha (who constitute more than 22.5% of the population) speak their own languages belonging to the Dravidian and Mundalanguage families.

Literature

The history of Odia literature has been mapped by historians along the following stages, Old Odia (900–1300 CE), Early Middle Odia (1300–1500 CE), Middle Odia (1500–1700 CE), Late Middle Odia (1700–1850 CE) and Modern Odia (from 1850 CE till the present). But this crude categorization could not skillfully draw the real picture on account of development and growth of Odia literature. Here, we split the total periods in different stages such as: Age of Charya Literature, Age of Sarala Das, Age of Panchasakha, Age of Upendra Bhanja, Age of Radhanath, Age of Satyabadi, Age of Marxism or Pragati yuga, Age of Romanticism or Sabuja Yuga, Post Independent Age.

The beginnings of Odia poetry coincide with the development of Charya Sahitya, the literature thus started by Mahayana Buddhist poets. This literature was written in a specific metaphor named "Sandhya Bhasha" and the poets like Luipa, Kanhupa are from the territory of Odisha.The language of Charya was considered as Prakrita.

The first great poet of Odisha is the famous Sarala Das who wrote the Mahabharata, not an exact translation from the Sanskrit original, but a full-blown independent work. *Sarala Mahabharat* has 152,000 verses compared to 100,000 in the Sanskrit version. Among many of his poems and epics, he is best remembered for his *Sarala Mahabharata. Chandi Purana* and the *Vilanka Ramayana* are also two of his famous creations. Arjuna Das, a contemporary to Sarala Das, wrote *Rama-Bibha*, a significant long poem in Odia.

Towards the 16th century, five poets emerged, though there are hundreds year gap in between them. But they are known as *Panchashakhas* as they believed in the same school of thought, *Utkaliya Vaishnavism*. The poets are: Balarama Dasa, Jagannatha Dasa, Achyutananada Dasa, Ananta Dasa and Jasobanta Das. The *Panchasakhas* are very much Vaishnavas by thought. In 1509, Chaitanya, an Odia devotee of Vishnu whose grandfather Madhukar Mishra had emigrated to Bengal, came to Odisha with his Vaishnava message of love. Before him Jayadeva, one of the foremost composers in Sanskrit, had prepared the ground by heralding the cult of Vaishnavism through his Gita Govinda. Chaitanya's path of devotion was known as *Raganuga Bhakti Marga*, but the *Panchasakhas* differed from Chaitanyas and believed in Gyana Mishra Bhakti Marga, which has similarities with the Buddhist philosophy of Charya Literature stated above. At the end of age of Panchasakha, the prominent poets are Dinakrushna Das, Upendra Bhanja and Abhimanyu Samanta Simhar. Verbal jugglery, obscenity and eroticism as the characteristics of Shringara Kavyas, became the trend of this period to which Upendra Bhanja took a leading role. His creations were Baidehisha Bilasa, Koti Brahmanda Sundari, Lavanyabati were proved landmark in Odia literature. Upendra Bhanja was conferred with the title *Kabi Samrat* of Odia literature for the aesthetic poetic sense and verbal jugglery proficiency. Dinakrushna Das's *Rasokallola* and Abhimanyu Samanta Simhara's *Bidagdha Chintamani* are prominent kavyas of this time.

The first Odia printing typeset was cast in 1836 by the Christian missionaries which heralded a great revolution in Odia literature, instead of palm leaf inscription. The books were being printed and the periodicals and journals were published. The first Odia Magazine of *Bodha Dayini* was published from Balasore in 1861. The main object of this magazine was to promote Odia literature and to draw attention to the lapses in government policy. The first Odia paper, *The Utkal Deepika* made its appearance in 1866 under the editorship of late Gouri Sankar Ray with the help of late Bichitrananda. The publication of these papers during the last part of the 19th century encouraged the modern literature and acted as a media to provide a wide readers range for the writers, The educated intellectuals came in contact with the English Literature and got influenced. Radhanath Ray (1849–1908) is the prime figure, who tried to write his poems with the influence of Western Literature. He wrote *Chandrabhaga, Nandikeshwari, Usha, Mahajatra, Darbar* and *Chilika* were the long poems or *Kavyas*. Fakir Mohan Senapati (1843–1918), the prime figure of modern Odia Fiction Prose is the product of that generation. He was considered the Vyasakabi or founder poet of Odia language. Fakir Mohan Senapati is well known for his novel *Chha Maana Atha Guntha*. It is the first Indian novel to deal with the exploitations of landless peasants by the Feudal Lords. It was written much before the October revolution of Russia or much before the emerging of marxist ideas in India.

With rise of freedom movement, a literary thought emerged with the influence of Gandhiji, and idealistic trend of Nationalism formed as a new trend in Odia literature. Much respected personality of Odishan culture and history, Utkalmani Gopabandhu Dash (1877–1928) had founded a school at a village Satyabadi near Sakshigopal of Odisha and an idealistic literary movement influenced the writers of this age. Godabarisha Mohapatra, Kuntala-Kumari Sabat are the other renowned names of this age.

With the emergence of soviet Russia in 1935, Communist party was formed in Odisha and a periodicals named *Adhunika* was published by the party. Bhagawati Charan Panigrahi and Sachidananda Routray were the founder member and writer/ poets of the party.

Bhagawati turned to a fiction writer and though Sachidananda Routray (who is more known as "Sachi Routra" or Sachi Babu) has written some of the short stories but was actually remembered for his poems. Influenced by the romantic thoughts of Rabindranath Tagore, during the thirties when the progressive marxian movements were in full flow in Odia literature, Kalindi Charan Panigrahi, the brother of Bhagabati Charan Panigrahi, the founder of Marxian Trend in Odisha, formed a group during 1920 called *Sabuja Samiti*.

Mayadhar Mansingh was a renowned poet of that time though he was considered as a romantic poet, but he kept the distance away from the influence of Rabindranath Tagore successfully. As the successor of Sachi babu, two poets Guruprasad Mohanty (popularly known as Guru Prasad) (1924–2004) and Bhanuji Rao came with T. S. Eliot and published their co-authored poetry book *Nutan Kabita*.

Later, Ramakanta Rath modified the ideas. Sitakanta Mohapatra, Soubhagya Kumar Mishra, Rajendra Kishore Panda, Brajanath Rath, Jayanta Mahapatra, Kamalakant Lenka, J. P. Das, Brahmotri Mohanty, Mamata Dash, Amaresh Patnaik, Hrushikesh Mallick, Sunil Kumar Prusty, Sucheta Mishra, Aparna Mohanty, Pritidhara Samal, Basudev Sunani, Gajanan Mishra, Bharat Majhi are some poets of this contemporary age.

In the Post-Independence era Odia fiction assumed a new direction. The trend which Fakir Mohan had started actually developed more after 1950s. Gopinath Mohanty (1914–1991), Surendra Mohanty and Manoj Das (b. 1934) are considered as three jewels of this time. The other significant fiction writers are Chandrasekhar Rath, Shantanu Acharya, Mohapatra Nilamani Sahoo, Rabi Patnaik, Jagadish Mohanty, Kanheilal Das, Satya Mishra, Ramchandra Behera, Padmaja Pal, Yashodhara Mishra and Sarojini Sahoo are few writers whose writings have created a new age in the field of fiction. After 1970, the women wing of Odia writers emerged as a prime voice of feminism.

Jayanti Ratha, Susmita Bagchi, Paramita Satpathy, Hiranmayee Mishra, Chirashree Indrasingh, Supriya Panda, Gayatri Saraf, Mamata Chowdhry are few fiction writer in this period. But, among all the women writers Sarojini Sahoo played a significant role for her feministic and sexuality approach in fiction. For feminism she is considered as the Simone de Beauvoirof India, though theoretically she denies the Hegelian theory of "Others" developed by Simone in her The Second Sex. Unlike to Simone, Sarojini claims the women are "Others" from masculine perspective but as a human being, she demands for similar right as Plato recommended.

In the field of drama, the traditional Odia theatre is the folk opera, or *Jatra*, which flourishes in the rural areas of Odisha. Modern theatre is no longer commercially viable. But in the 1960, experimental theatre made a mark through the works of Manoranjan Das, who pioneered the new theatre movement with his brand of experimentalism. Bijay Mishra, Biswajit Das, Kartik Rath, Ramesh Chandra Panigrahi, Ratnakar Chaini, Ranjit Patnaik continued the tradition.

PERFORMING ARTS

Music

Sixteenth century witnessed the compilation of literature on music. The four important treatises written during that time are Sangitarnava Chandrika, Natya Manorama, Sangita Kalpalata and Gita Prakasha. Odissi music is a combination of four distinctive kinds of music, namely, Chitrapada, Dhruvapada, Panchali and Chitrakala. When music uses artwork, it is known as *Chitrakala*. A unique feature of Odia music is the *Padi*, which consists of singing of words in fast beat.

Being a part of the rich culture of Odisha, its music is also as much charming and colorful. Odissi music is more two thousand five hundred years old and comprises a number of categories. Of these, the five broad ones are Tribal Music, Folk music, Light Music, Light-Classical Music and Classical Music. Anyone who is trying to understand the culture of Odisha must take into account its music, which essentially forms a part of its legacy.

In the ancient times, there were saint-poets who wrote the lyrics of poems and songs that were sung to rouse the religious feelings of people. It was by the eleventh century that the music of Odisha, in the form of Triswari, Chatuhswari, and Panchaswari, underwent transformation and was converted into the classical style.

Folk music like *Jogi Gita, Kendara Gita, Dhuduki Badya, Prahallada Nataka, Palla, Sankirtan, Mogal Tamasa, Gitinatya, Kandhei Nacha, Kela Nacha, Ghoda Nacha, Danda Nacha* and *Daskathia* are popular in Odisha.

Almost every tribal group has their own distinct song and dance style.

Dance

Odissi dance and music are classical forms. Odissi has a tradition of 2,000 years, and finds mention in the *Natyashastra* of Bharatamuni, possibly written circa 200 BCE. However, the dance form nearly became extinct during the British period, only to be revived after India's independence by a few proponents, such as Guru Deba Prasad Das, Guru Pankaj Charan Das, Guru Raghunath Dutta and Kelucharan Mohapatra. Odissi classical dance is about the divine love of Krishna and his consort Radha, mostly drawn from compositions by the notable Odia poet Jayadeva, who lived in the 12th century CE.

Chhau dance (or Chau dance) is a form of tribal martial dance attributed to origins in Mayurbhanj princely state of Odisha and seen in the Indian states of West Bengal, Jharkhand and Odisha. There are three subtypes of the dance, based on the original places where the subtypes were developed.

Seraikella Chau was developed in Seraikella, the administrative head of the Seraikela Kharsawan district of Jharkhand, *Purulia Chau* in Purulia district of West Bengal and *Mayurbhanj Chau* in Mayurbhanj district of Odisha.

Mahari Dance is one of the important dance forms of Odisha. Mahari dance, originated in the temples of Odisha. History of Odisha provides evidence of the *Devadasi* cult in Odisha. Devadasis were dancing girls who were dedicated to the temples of Odisha. The Devadasis in Odisha were known as *Maharis* and the dance performed by them came to be known as *Mahari Dance*.

It was during the reign of Chodagangadeva, Maharis were employed in the temples of Puri. After Chodagangadeva's death, Ananabhimadeva built Natyamandapa in the Jagannath temple for the dance performances inside the temple. Moreover, in those days, the Mahari dancers belonged to different categories namely, the *Nachunis* (dancers), the *Bahara Gauni*, the *Bhitara Gauni* and the *Gaudasanis*.

The Mahari Dancers of Odisha are supposed to follow certain restrictions, such as:

- They should dance on the ceremonies connected to Lord Jagannath.
- They should adhere to the specifications made by the Shastras.
- They must always wear clean clothes.
- The dancer cannot be physically handicapped.
- At the time of the performances, the dancers are not supposed to look at the audience.
- The Maharis are married to the Lord at the age of nine.
- Before their performances, the Mahari dancers pay their obeisance to the Lord.

In Odisha, one can also come across another type of Mahari dancers, who are known as *Samarpada Niyoga*. The duty of the *Samarpada Niyoga* is to dance during the ceremonial procession of the deities. These dancers perform during the Ratha Yatra, Jhulana Yatra, Dola Yatra, etc.

Western Odisha has also great variety of dance forms unique to Odisha culture. The children's verses are known as "Chhiollai", "Humobauli" and "Doligit"; the adolescent poems are "Sajani", "Chhata", "Daika", "Bhekani"; the youth compositions are "Rasarkeli", "Jaiphul", "Maila Jada", "Bayamana", "Gunchikuta" and "Dalkhai"; the work-man's poetry comprises "Karma" and "Jhumer" pertaining to Lord Vishwakarma and the "Karamashani" Goddess. The professional entertainers perform Dand, Danggada, Mudgada, Ghumra, Sadhana, Sabar–Sabarein, Disdigo, Nachina–Bajnia, Samparda and Sanchar. They are performed during all occasions with varieties of rhythm and rhyme.

Pala is a unique form of balladry in Odisha, which artistically combines elements of theatre, classical Odissi music, highly refined Odia and Sanskrit poetry, wit, and humour. The literal meaning of *Pala* is turn. It is more sophisticated than the other Odia ballad tradition, *Daskathia*. *Pala* can be presented in three different ways. First one is known as *Baithaki Pala* or 'seated', in which the performers sit on the ground throughout. The other one is *Thia Pala* or 'standing', which is considerably more popular and aesthetically more satisfying. The third one is called the *Badi Pala*, which is a kind of *Thia Pala*, in which two groups vie for excellence. This is the most entertaining, as there is an element of competition.

Gotipua dance is another form of dance in Odisha. In Odia colloquial language Gotipua means single boy. The dance performance done by a single boy is known as Gotipua dance. When decadence and declination came in to *Devadasi* or *Mahari* tradition due to various reasons this Gotipua dance tradition evolved as sequel as these performance were practiced to please God. It is totally unknown that when exactly this danced form came in to practice. Still some historians say that this dance tradition appears to have originated during the region of Prataprudradev (1497 CE to 1540 CE) and gained popularity in the subsequent Muslim rule. Ray Remananda the famous Vaishnavite Minister of King Pratapruda and ardent follower of Sri Chaitanya is the originator of this boy dancing tradition, as the Vasishnavas were not approving of the females in to dance practices so it possible that the dance tradition must have come after Sri Chaitanya came to Odisha. The Gotipua Dance Tradition is now seen in the village Raghurajpur situated 10 km away from Puri town, situated on the banks of river Bhargabi. It is otherwise known as the Crafts Village as various Odishan handicrafts' craftsmen reside in this village contributing their expertise in Pattachitra painting and other handicrafts.

Jhumair is a folk dance from North and Western Odisha. It is perfermed during harvest season and festivals.

Odia cinema

The Odia film production in the initial years was very slow. After first Odia film Sita Bibaha, only two films were produced till 1951. A joint consortium of landlords and businessmen who collected fund after 1948 produced those two movies. The 1951 production Roles to Eight was the first Odia film having an English name. It was released after 15 years of the first Odia film Sita Bibaha. It was the fourth Odia film produced by Ratikanta Padhi. The eleventh Odia film Sri Lokenath was the first Odia film, which got National Award in 1960 directed by Prafulla Sengupta.

The name of Prashanta Nanda would always come while dealing with Odia Film Industry. He was present in Odia films since 1939, but he became super active only after 1976. Nanda served Odia Film Industry as an actor, director, screenplay writer, and lyricist and even as a playback singer. Such a versatile genius is quite rare in Indian cinema history. Uttam Mohanty, whose debut film *Abhiman* won accolades, was one of the ruling heroes of the Odia Film Industry. His wife Aparajita Mohanty is a very successful leading lady of Odia films.

ODIA CUISINE

Odisha has culinary tradition spanning centuries if not millennia. The kitchen of the famous Jagannath temple in Puri is reputed to be the largest in the world, with a thousand chefs, working around 752 wood-burning clay hearths called chulas, to feed over 10,000 people each day. Rasagolla, one of the most popular desserts in India, is an estrangment between the Odisha and West Bengal. It had been enjoyed in Odisha for centuries and neighboring Bengal. The well-known rice pudding, kheeri (kheer) that is relished all over India.

In fact, some well-known recipes, usually credited to Bengal, are of Odishan origin. This is because during the Bengal renaissance, Brahmin cooks from Odisha, especially from Puri, were routinely employed in richer Bengali households. They were famed for their culinary skills and commonly referred to as Ude Thakurs (Odia Brahmin-cooks). As a result, many Odia delicacies got incorporated into the Bengali kitchen.

Chena Poda is another famous sweet delicacy in Odisha with the origin from Nayagarh Disctrict, Odisha

Pakhala, a dish made of rice, water, and yoghurt, that is fermented overnight, is very popular in summer, particularly in the rural areas. Odias are very fond of sweets and no Odia repast is considered complete without some dessert at the end. A typical meal in Odisha consists of a main course and dessert. Typically breads are served as the main course for breakfast, whereas rice is eaten with lentils (dals) during lunch and dinner. The main course also includes one or more curries, vegetables and pickles. Given the fondness for sweet foods, the dessert course may include generous portions of more than a single item. Odia desserts are made from a variety of ingredients, with milk, chhenna (a form of ricotta cheese), coconut, rice, and wheat flour being the most common.

Clothing

Western-style dress has gained greater acceptance in cities and towns among men, although the people prefer to wear traditional dresses like Dhoti, Kurtha and Gamucha during festivals or other religious occasions. Women normally prefer to wear the Sari (Sambalpuri Sari,) or the Shalwar kameez; western attire is becoming popular among younger women in cities and towns.

The Saree of Odisha is much in demand throughout the entire world. The different colors and varieties of sarees in Odisha make them very popular among the women of the state. The handloom sarees available in Odisha can be of four major types; these are *Sambalpui Ikat*, *Sambalpuri Bandha*, *Sambalpuri Bomkai* and *Sambalpuri Saptaper*. Odisha sarees are also available in other colors like cream, maroon, brown and rust. The *tie-and-dye* technique used by the weavers of Odisha to create motifs on these sarees is unique to this region. This technique also gives the sarees of Odisha an identity of their own.

ODISSI MUSIC

Odissi music *iúî*) is a genre of classical music in India originated from the eastern state of Odisha. Indian classical music has five significant branches: Avanti, Panchali, Odramagadhi, Hindustani and Carnatic. Of these, Odramagadhi exists in the form of Odissi music. Generally, Odissi is one of the classical dances of India performed with Odissi music. Odissi music was shaped during the time of Odiya poet Jayadeva, who composed lyrics meant to be sung. By the 11th century AD, folk music of Odisha in the form of Triswari, Chatuhswari, and Panchaswari was modified into the classical style. However, Odissi songs were written even before the Oriya language developed. Odissi music has a rich legacy dating back to the 2nd century BCE, when king Kharvela, the ruler of Odisha (Kalinga), patronized this music and dance.

Origin and history

Ancient Odisha had a rich culture of music, which is substantiated by many archaeological excavation throughout Odisha. At Sankarjung in the Angul district, the initial spade work exposed the cultural stratum of the Chalcolitic period. From here, polished stone celts and hand-made pottery have been excavated. Some of the Celts are narrow but large in size. Thus they are described as Bar-celts. On the basis of bar-celts discovered in Sankarjung it could be argued that they were an earlier musical instrument in India. There is historical evidence in the form of sculptural evidence, i.e. musical instruments, singing and dancing postures of damsels in the Ranigumpha Caves in Khandagiri and Udayagiri at Bhubaneswar.

Charya Geetika (poems of Buddhist literature), written between 7th to 12th century mostly by the poets of Odisha and Bengal, are connected with Tantric Buddhism. All India literature on music like Bharat Muni's Natya Shastra, written in 2nd to 4th century AD., referred to the Odra Magadhi style of music and dance, which belonged to Odisha. Similarly, Sangeet Ratnakar also had a reference to the Odra Magadhi style of music. There are certain texts on Odissi music which are authentic and authoritative, and are excellent indices to the development of the music. These are written in Sanskrit or Oriya and contain the characteristics of Udramagadhi, Ardhamagadhi, Udra Bhasa and Utkalika Bibhasa. These were Oriya Charyagitika by different Oriya Sidhacharyas in the 7th to 11th centuries, Gita Govinda by Sri Jayadeva in the 12th century, Sangita Sara by Hari Nayak in the 14th century to 15th century, Rasavaridhi by Brundavan Das in the 15th century, Oriya Mahabharata by Sarala Das in the 15th century, Rasakallola by Dinakrushna Das in the 16th century, etc. Other books written in later years were Sangita Darpana, Sangit Kalpadruma, Sangitarnava Chandrika, Baidehisha Vilash, etc. It proves that Odissi music is more ancient than its counterparts like Hindustani or Carnatic

Even Mahari tradition and singing of Geeta-Govinda in the temple of Lord Jagannath since the time of King Pratap Rudra Dev in the 15th century proves the rich tradition of Odissi. In the temples of Odisha of 7th and 13th century AD such as Parsuramesvar, Muktesvara, Lingaraj and Konark, there are engravings depicting musical performances and dancing postures.

After the reign of Mukund Dev in the 16th century AD., Odissi music suffered during the Maratha rule in Odisha during the 17th and 18th century AD. It also did not flourish during the British Raj.

Characteristics

Jayadeva, the saint-poet, the great composer and illustrious master of classical music, has immense contribution to Odissi music. During his time Odra-Magadhi style music got shaped and achieved its classical status. He indicated the classical ragas prevailing at that time in which these were to be sung. Prior to that there was the tradition of Chhanda which was simple in musical outline. From the 16th century onwards, treatises on music were Sangitamava Chandrika, Gita Prakasha, Sangita Kalalata and Natya Manorama. A couple of treatise namely, *Sangita Sarani* and *Sangi Narayana*, were also written in the early path of the 19th century.

Odissi Sangita comprises four classes of music namely Dhruvapada, Chitrapada, Chitrakala and Panchal, described in the above-mentioned texts. The chief Odissi *and Shokabaradi. Odissi Sangita (music) is a synthesis of four classes of music, i.e. Dhruvapada, Chitrapada, Chitrakala and Panchal, described in the above-mentioned texts. The Dhruvapada is the first line or lines to be sung repeatedly. Chitrapada means the arrangement of words in an alliterative style. The use of art in music is called Chitrakala. Kavisurya Baladev Rath, the renowned Oriya poet wrote lyrics, which are the best examples of Chitrakala. All of these were* Chhanda (metrical section) contains the essence of Odissi music. The Chhandas were composed by combining Bhava (theme), Kala (time), and Swara(tune). The Chautisha represents the originality of Odissi style. All the thirty four (34) letters of the Oriya alphabet from 'Ka' to 'Ksha'are used chronologically at the beginning of each line.

A special feature of Odissi music is the padi which consists of words to be sung in Druta Tala (fast beat). Odissi music can be sung to different talas: Navatala (nine beats), Dashatala (ten beats) or Egartala (eleven beats). Odissi ragas are different from the ragas of Hindustani and Karnataki classical music. The primary Odissi ragas are Kalyana, Nata, Shree Gowda, Baradi, Panchama, Dhanashri, Karnata, Bhairavee and Shokabaradi.

Odissi music is sung through Raganga, Bhabanga and Natyanga Dhrubapadanga followed by Champu, Chhanda, Chautisa, Pallabi, Bhajan, Janana, and Gita Govinda, which are considered to be a part of the repertoire of Odissi or an allied act form of Odissi.

Odissi music has codified grammars, which are presented with specified Raagas. It has also a distinctive rendition style. It is lyrical in its movement with wave-like ornamentation. The pace of singing in Odissi is not very fast nor too slow, and it maintains a proportional tempo which is very soothing.

The great exponents of Odissi music in modern times are the Late Singhari Shyamasundar Kar, Markeandeya Mahapatra, Kashinath Pujapanda, Balakirshan Das, Gopal Chandra Panda,Ramhari Das,Bhubaneswari Misra, Shymamani Devi and Sunanda Patnaik, who have achieved eminence in classical music.

Relation with other classical music

The percussion instrument played with Odissi music is the 'Mardal'. Temple sculptures in Odisha abound in statues of 'Mardal' players. At one time the Kalinga Empire extended all the way up to the river Kaveri and incorporated major parts of Karnataka.

King Purusottama Deba of Odisha conquered Kanchi and married the princess. There were many singers from South India in the courts of Odisha. The main singer of the compositions of Kavisurya was Rajamani, a Telugu weaver. The interaction between Odisha and South India led to the widespread singing of Jayadeva's Astapadis in South Odisha in typical Carnatic style of music. Some raagas specific to Odisha are "Desakhya", "Dhanasri", "Belabali", "Kamodi", "Baradi" etc. Additionally, some Odissi raagas bear the same names as Hindustani or Carnatic raagas, but have different note combinations. Furthermore, there are many raagas that have the same note combinations in Hindustani, Carnatic and Odissi styles, but are called by different names. Some examples are — Raaga

"Durga" in Hindustani is the same as raaga "Sudha Saveri" in Carnatic style is the same as raaga "Kamodi" in Odissi style. In fact, the Hindustani raaga "Chandrakauns" could have developed from the Odissi raaga "Lalita". Each stream, however, has its own distinct style of rendition and tonal development despite the apparent similarity in scale.

Nature of Odissi music composition

A good Odissi music composition must have following characteristics, 1.Varitation of beat and pause. 2.Use of "gamak" or "Andolan". 3."Matu" meaning lucid presentation of composition. 4.Efficient and pleasing expansion of the "Raaga" and "Geeta". 5.Lucid and Melodious rendering of "Taan". 6.Singing of special words and notes with novelty. 7.Avoiding repetition of same notes or compositions. 8.Every sentence rendered with its unique quality, beautification and melody.

Odissi music in modern time

The great exponents of Odissi music in modern times are the Late Singhari Shyamasundar Kar, Markeandeya Mahapatra, Kashinath Pujapanda, Balakirshan Das, Bhubaneswari Misra, Shymamani Devi, Gopal Panda, Padmashree Raghunath Panigrahi, Ramahari Das, Laxmikant Palit and Sunanda Patnaik, who have achieved eminence in classical music.

In order to popularize the Odissi music the State Government's Culture Department has undertaken a massive programme named 'Odissi Sandhya' to be performed in all major cities of the country.

The programme is being executed through Guru Kelu Charan Mohapatra Odissi Research Centre in association with different cultural organizations located in different parts of the country, like Central Sangeet Natak Academy, Eastern Zonal Cultural Centre, Kolkata, and Prachhin Kalakendra, Chandigarh. Programmes held at Chandigarh and New Delhi have already started creating a mild sensation among the music lovers of the country.

CUISINE OF ODISHA

Compared to other regional Indian cuisines, Odia cuisine uses less oil and is less spicy while nonetheless remaining flavourful. Rice is the staple food of this region. Mustard oil is used in some dishes as the cooking medium, but ghee (made of cow's milk) is preferred in temples. In old times food was traditionally served on banana leaves or disposable plates made of salleaves.

Odia cooks, particularly from the Puri region, were much sought after due to their ability to cook food in accordance with Hindu scriptures. During the 19th century, many Odia cooks were employed in Bengal and they took many Odia dishes with them. This period also saw a heavy demand for Brahmin cooks, leading many Odia cooks to fake their castes.

Yoghurt is used in dishes. Many sweets of the region are based on *chhena* (cheese).

Ingredients and seasoning

The ingredients used in Odia cuisine are plantains, jackfruit, and papaya. The curries are garnished with dried raw mango (*ambula*) .

Panch phutana is a blend of five spices that is widely used in Odia cuisine. It contains mustard, cumin, fenugreek, aniseed and kalonji. Garlic, onion and ginger are used in most of the food. Temple food preparation doesn't allow the use of garlic or onion. Turmeric and red chillies are used regularly

Local variation

The food in the region around Puri-Cuttack is greatly influenced by the Jagannath Temple. On the other hand, kalonji and mustard paste are used mostly in the region bordering Bengal and curries tend to be sweeter. In the region closer to Andhra Pradesh, curry tree leaves and tamarind are used more. The Brahmapur region has influences of South Indian cuisine and the Telugu people living there have invented new Odia dishes.

Temple food

Abadha, *the afternoon meal of the Jagannath Temple served on a plantain leaf.*

Temples in the region make offerings to the presiding deities. The *prasada* of the Jagannath Temple is well known and is specifically called Maha Prasad meaning greatest of all prasadas. It consists of 56 recipes, so it is called *chhapan bhoga*. It is based on the legend that Krishna missed his eight meals for seven days while trying to save a village from a storm holding up the Govardhan hill as a shelter.

Fish and seafood

Fish and other seafoods are eaten mainly in coastal areas. Several curries are prepared from prawn and lobster with spices. Freshwater fishis available from rivers and irrigation canals. Rohu, Catla and Ilishi are the famous freshwater fishes used in curries.

List of dishes

Rice dishes and rotis

- *Pakhala* is a rice dish made by adding water to cooked rice. It may then be allowed to ferment overnight. This is called *basi pakhala*. The unfermented version of this is called *saja pakhala*. It is served with green chillies, onions, yoghurt, badi etc. It is primarily eaten in summer.

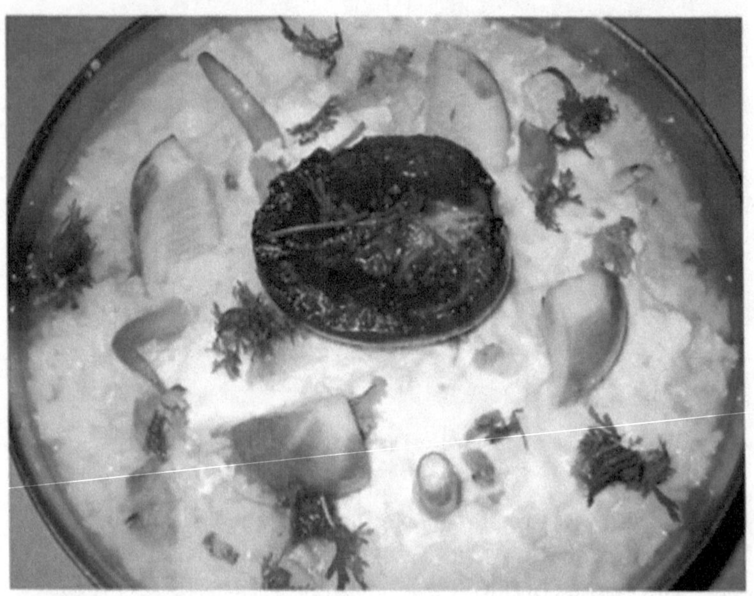

Pakhala *served with wads of lemon, yoghurt and a slice of tomato.*

- *Khechidi* is a rice dish cooked with lentils. It is the Odia version of *khichdi*.

- *Palau* is a rice dish made from vegetables and raisins. It is the Odia version of *pilaf*.

- *Kanika* is a sweet rice dish, garnished with raisins and nuts.

- *Ghee rice* is fried with ghee and cinnamon

Dal

- *Dalma*: A dish made from dal and vegetables. It is generally made from toor dal and contains chopped vegetables like green papaya, unripe banana, eggplant, pumpkin, gourd, etc. It is garnished with turmeric, mustard seeds, and panch phutana. There are several variations of this dish.

- *Dali* : A dish made from one of the Dals like tur, chana, masur, mung or a combination of these.

Curries

Odia cooking has some different type of curries based on the overall preparation style. Tarakari, Santula, Rai, Rasa.

- *Santula*: A dish of finely chopped vegetables which are sauteed with garlic, green chilies, mustard and spices. It has several variations.
- *Chaatu rai*: A dish made from mushrooms and mustard.
- *Alu potala rosa*: Curry made from potato and parval.
- *Kadali manja rai*: A curry made from banana plant stem and mustard seeds. *Manja* refers to the stem which can be used in *dalma*.
- *Mahura*
- *Besara*: Assorted vegetables in mustard paste tempered with panch phutana

Khattas and chutneys

Khatta refers to a type of sour side dish or chutney usually served with Odia thalis.

- *Dahi baigana*: A sour dish made from yoghurt and eggplants.
- *Khajuri khata*: A sweet-and-sour dish made from tomato and dates.
- *Amba khatta*: A *khatta* made from raw mangoes.
- *Ouu khatta*: Elephant apple *khatta*
- *Dhania-patra chutney*: A chutney made from coriander leaves.

Saaga (salad greens)

In Odia cuisine, sâga is one of the most important vegetables. It is popular all over the state. A list of the plants that are used as sâga is as below. Odias typically eat lots of cooked green leaves. They are prepared by adding "pancha phutana", with or without onion/garlic, and are best enjoyed with pakhala.

- Kalama sâga Ipomoea aquatica (Water Spinach)
- Kosalâ/Khadâ sâga: prepared from amaranth leaves.
- Bajji sâga: Prepared from Amaranthus dubius leaves.
- Leutiâ sâga Amaranthus viridis leaves and tender stems.
- Pâlanga sâga spinach
- Poi sâga: prepared from basella leaves and tender stems.
- Bâramâsi/Sajanâ sâga: prepared from leaves of the drumstick tree. Cooked with lentils or alone with fried onions.
- Sunusuniâ sâga Marsilea polycarpa leaves.
- Pitâgama sâga
- Pidanga sâga
- Kakhâru sâga: Prepared from leaves of the pumpkin plant.
- Madarangâ sâga: prepared from leaves of Alternanthera sessilis.
- Sorisa saga: Mustard greens
- Methi sâga: prepared from methi or Fenugreek leaves and besara (mustard paste) cooked with vegetable.
- Matara sâga: The inner coating of peas is removed and then chopped to make the saga.

One of the most popular is lali koshala saaga made from green leaves with red stems.Other saagas that are eaten are pita gahama, khada, poi, koshala, sajana etc. Some items are as follows;

- Saaga Bhaja
- Saaga Muga
- Saaga Baadi
- Saaga Rai
- Saru patra tarkari

Pithas (sweet cakes)

Pithas and sweets are types of traditional Odia dishes.
- Podo pitha

- Enduri Pitha
- Arisa Pitha
- Kakara Pitha
- Manda Pitha
- Chakuli Pitha
- Tal Pitha
- Chitau Pitha
- Parijata Pitha
- Nurukhurum Pitha
- Chandrakanti
- Chhunchi Patra Pitha
- Goitha goli Pitha
- Haldi Patra Pitha
- Lau Pitha
- Muan

Egg, chicken and mutton

- Egg tarkari: An egg curry prepared with onion and tomato paste
- Chicken tarkari: A chicken curry
- Chicken kasa
- Mangsha tarkari
- Mangsha kasa

Fish and other sea food

- *Machha Besara*: A fish curry prepared with mustard paste.
- *Machha Mahura*: A curry prepared with fish and vegetables.
- Machha Jhola
- Chingudi Jhola
- Dahi machha
- Machha chhencheda | Mudhi Ghanta

- Chunna Machha Jhola: A fish curry, similar to Machha Jhola, but prepared with small smelt fish.
- Chunna Machha Tarkari: Small fried smelt fishes
- Chingudi Malai Tarkari: A prawn curry
- Kankada Jhola: Crab curry
- Chingudi chadchadi
- Kokali sukhua rai

Fritters and fries

- Alloo piaji: A savory snack, similar to pakora or fritters, made with potatoes and onions, long-sliced, mixed and dipped in a batter of gram-flour, and then deep-fried
- Bhendi baigana bhaja: okra (ladies' fingers) and eggplant, sliced and deep-fried
- Badi Chura: A coarse crushed mixture of sun-dried lentil dumplings (*Badi*), onion, gralic, green chillies and mustard oil
- Pampad : flat savory snack like deep-friend or roasted appetizer, which looks very similar to a roti, usually eaten during lunch time
- Phula badi: Bigger and inflated versions of the normal *Badi* - a sun-dried lentil dumpling
- Sajana Chhuin Bhaja: Drumsticks sliced into 3 to 3 inch long pieces and deep/shallow fried in oil

Snacks

- *Ghugni*: A spicy dish made from peas, can be served with *pooris*.
- phuchuka
- Chaat
- Dohibara Alludum
- Chanachura or Baramaza
- Piaji
- Bara
- Gulgula

- Checha Piaji
- Kachodi chaat
- Suji Bara
- Pakudi
- Aloo chop
- Baigani
- Dantikili

Desserts and sweets

- Kheeri: Kheeri is the Odia word for kheer, predominantly made of rice.
- Chhena Poda: A sweet made from soft cheese dipped in sugar syrup and baked. It may contain dry fruits.
- Chhena Gajja
- Malpua
- Kora
- Khira sagara
- Khirsapani
- Chhena kheeri
- Chhena Jhili
- Rasagola
- Rasabali
- Rasmalei
- Aadasi
- Attakali
- Khaja
- Magaj Ladu
- Gajja : a light savory snack
- Rabidi : a sweet curd like dish
- Mudki:A famous savory snack which looks very similar to that of a jalebi but the only difference being that jalebi are on the sweet palete where as mudki are light and in the savory side
- Chenna Mudki.

CINEMA OF ODISHA

The Odia film industry, colloquially known as Ollywood, is the Odia language Indian film industry, based in Cuttack, Odisha. The name is a portmanteau of the words Odia and Hollywood.

Industry

In 1974, the Government of Odisha declared film making and construction of cinema theaters as an industry in the state, and in 1976 it established the Odisha Film Development Corporation in Cuttack.

Highest grossing odia movies

1. Prem Kumar:9.94 crore
2. Tokata Fasigala:9.10 crore
3. Something Something:8.50 crore
4. Kabula Barabula:8.35 crore
5. Agastya:8.10 crore
6. Abhaya:7.30 crore
7. Ishq Puni Thare:7.05 crore
8. Balunga Toka:7 crore
9. Ishq Tu Hi Tu:6.79 crore
10. Sriman Surdas:6.35 crore
11. Sundergarh Ra Salman Khan:6.30 crore
12. Pilata Bigidigala:6.25 crore
13. I Love You:6.20 crore
14. Hero No 1:6.10 crore
15. Super Michhua:5.98 crore

History

Oriya has a history of filmmaking, starting in 1936. The first Oriya production, a talkie, *Sita Bibaha*, was made by Mohan Sundar Deb Goswami in 1936. Drawn from the Indian epic *Ramayana*, the story is about the marriage of Sita and

Ram. The film plot was made from a drama written by Kamapala Mishra. Prepared with a budget of only Rs 30,000, the film has 14 song sequences. Despite it being the first Oriya film with several drawbacks in every section of its making, the two-hour-long movie generated great enthusiasm among the people. It was released by Laksmi Talkies, Puri. The 12-reeled film had in its cast Makhanlal Banerjee (Ram), who received only Rs 120 for his performance, Aditya Ballav Mohanty (Lakhsman), who got only Rs 35 as conveyance allowance, and Prabati Devi (Sita), who was paid the highest amount of Rs 150. This was a landmark film of the Oriya film Industry.

The pace of Oriya film production in the initial years was very slow. After *Sita Bibaha*, only two films were produced until 1951. A joint consortium of landlords and businessmen who collected funds after 1948 produced those two movies. The 1951 production *Roles to Eight* was the first Oriya film with an English name. It was released 15 years after the first Oriya film, *Sita Bibaha*. It was the fourth Oriya film produced by Ratikant Padhi.

The eleventh Oriya film, *Sri Lokenath*, was directed by Prafulla Sengupta and received the National Award in 1960.

The same year, Prasanta Nanda won the National Film Award for Best Feature Film in Oriya for his debut film, *Nua Bou*. His name would always be synonymous with the Oriya film industry. He was present in Oriya films since 1939, but he became very active only after 1976. Nanda was an actor, director, screenplay writer, lyricist and playback singer. Nanda won National Awards three times, in 1960, 1966 and 1969 for his acting in *Nua Bou*, *Matir Manisha* and *Adina Megha*.

Mohammad Mohsin started the revolution in the Oriya film industry by not only securing the essence of the Oriya culture but also changing the way the film industry watched Oriya movies. *Phoola Chandana* was written by Ananda Sankar Das. He belongs to Cuttack. His movies heralded the golden era of the Oriya film industry by bringing in freshness to Oriya movies. His directorial debut was *Phoola Chandana* for which he won the Odisha State Film Award for Best Director. He had to his credit 16 box office successful movies in his directorial stint. He started as an actor in character roles and gave household names like Raaka to Odisha.

Amiya Ranjan Patnaik, who started his career directing *Mamata Mage Mula*, changed the dimension of the Oriya film industry by producing big budget movies with multiple star casts, which was a new trend at that time. He introduced many newcomers, musicians, technicians and singers from Mumbai and Chennai. He also produced the National Award-winning film *Hakim Babu* in 1985. His film *Pua Mora Kala Thakura*, directed by Raju Mishra, was one of the biggest successes in the Oriya film industry, followed by *Chaka Aakhi Sabu Dekhuchi* and *Asuchi Mo Kalia Suna*. He frequently collaborated with Raju Mishra, Akshaya Mohanty, Bijay Mohanty and Uttam Mohanty. He started the trend of producing trilingual films in the Oriya film industry. *Raja Rani*, *Paradeshi Babu* and *Parimahal* were made in Oriya, Bengali and Bangladeshi. He made a comeback as a director and made Tulasi Apa produced by his son Anupam Patnaik. Tulasi Apa was a critical success within many international festivals. This was the first biopic of Odisha based on Padmashree Tulasi Munda.

Uttam Mohanty, whose debut film *Abhiman* won accolades, was very successful in the 1990s. His wife Aparajita Mohanty is also an actress. Actress Nandita Das, who acted in several Hindi movies like *Fire,* has an Oriya origin. She acted in the Susanta Misra-directed *Biswaprakash*, which won a National Award in 2000. Critics have named Bijay Mohantyand Mihir Das to be two of the best Oriya actors so far. Siddhanta Mahapatra, a new generation star, is also successful. Barsha Priyadarshini is also another successful actress in the millennium era of Oriya cinema. Anubhab Mohanty is a well-known name in Ollywood, famous for his action and romantic movies. Mrinal Sen directed an Oriya film, Matira Manisha, which won a National Film Award for Best Feature Film in Oriya to Prashanta Nanda.

3

Government and Politics

INTRODUCTION

All states in India are governed by a parliamentary system of government based on universal adult franchise. India's parliament is bicameral. The lower house is called the Lok Sabha. Odisha contributes 21 members to Lok Sabha. They are directly elected by the electorates. The upper house is called the Rajya Sabha. Odisha contributes 10 members to Rajya Sabha. They are elected by the state's legislature.

Odisha State Secretariat building in Bhubaneswar

The main parties active in the politics of Odisha are the Biju Janata Dal, the Indian National Congress and Bhartiya Janata Party. Following the Odisha State Assembly Election in 2014, the Naveen Patnaik-led Biju Janata Dal stayed in power for the fourth consecutive term.

Legislative assembly

The Odisha state has a unicameral legislature. The Odisha Legislative Assembly consists of 147 elected members, and special office bearers such as the Speaker and Deputy Speaker, who are elected by the members. Assembly meetings are presided over by the Speaker, or by the Deputy Speaker in the Speaker's absence. Executive authority is vested in the Council of Ministers headed by the Chief Minister, although the titular head of government is the Governor of Odisha. The Governor is appointed by the President of India. The leader of the party or coalition with a majority in the Legislative Assembly is appointed as the Chief Minister by the Governor, and the Council of Ministers are appointed by the Governor on the advice of the Chief Minister. The Council of Ministers reports to the Legislative Assembly. The 147 elected representatives are called Members of the Legislative Assembly, or MLAs. One MLA may be nominated from the Anglo-Indian community by the Governor. The term of the office is for 5 years, unless the Assembly is dissolved prior to the completion of the term.

Administrative units

There are 30 districts in Odisha — Angul, Balangir, Balasore, Bargarh, Bhadrak, Boudh, Cuttack, Deogarh, Dhenkanal, Gajapati, Ganjam, Jagatsinghpur, Jajpur, Jharsuguda, Kandhamal, Kalahandi, Kendrapara, Keonjhar, Khordha, Koraput, Malkangiri, Mayurbhanj, Nabarangpur, Nayagarh, Nuapada, Puri, Rayagada, Sambalpur, Subarnapur, Sundargarh.

These 30 districts have been placed under three different revenue divisions to streamline their governance. The divisions are North, South and Central, with their headquarters at

Sambalpur, Berhampur and Cuttack respectively. Each division consists of 10 districts, and has as its administrative head a Revenue Divisional Commissioner (RDC). The position of the RDC in the administrative hierarchy is that between that of the district administration and the state secretariat. The RDCs report to the Board of Revenue, which is headed by a senior officer of the Indian Administrative Service.

Each district is governed by a *Collector & District Magistrate*, who is appointed from the Indian Administrative Service. The Collector & District Magistrate is responsible for collecting the revenue and maintaining law and order in the district.

Each District is separated into Sub-Divisions, each governed by a *Sub-Collector and Sub-Divisional Magistrate*. The Sub-Divisions are further divided into Tahasils. The Tahasils are headed by *Tahasildar*. Odisha has 58 Sub-Divisions, 317 Tahasils and 314 Blocks. Blocks consists of Panchayats (village councils) and town municipalities.

The capital and largest city of the state is Bhubaneswar. The other major cities are Cuttack, Rourkela, Berhampur and Sambalpur. Municipal Corporations in Odisha include Bhubaneswar, Cuttack, Berhampur, Sambalpur and Rourkela.

Other municipalities of Odisha include Angul, Balangir, Balasore, Barbil, Bargarh, Baripada, Belpahar, Bhadrak, Bhawanipatna, Biramitrapur, Boudh, Byasanagar, Chhatrapur, Deogarh, Dhenkanal, Gopalpur, Gunupur, Jagatsinghpur, Jajpur, Jeypore, Jharsuguda, Joda, Kendrapara, Kendujhar, Khordha, Konark, Koraput, Malkangiri, Nabarangpur, Nayagarh, Nuapada, Paradeep, Paralakhemundi, Phulbani, Puri, Rajgangpur, Rayagada, Sonepur, Sundargarh, Talcher and Umerkote.

Auxiliary authorities known as panchayats, for which local body elections are regularly held, govern local affairs.

The judiciary is composed of the Odisha High Court, located at Cuttack, and a system of lower courts.

GOVERNMENT OF ODISHA

The Government of Odisha and its 30 districts consists of an executive, led by the Governor of Odisha, a judiciary, and a legislative branch.

Like other states in India, the head of state of Odisha is the Governor, appointed by the President of India on the advice of the Central government. His or her post is largely ceremonial. The Chief Minister is the head of government and is vested with most of the executive powers. Bhubaneswar is the capital of Odisha, and houses the Vidhan Sabha (Legislative Assembly) and the secretariat. The Orissa High Court, located in Cuttack, has jurisdiction over the whole state.

The present Legislative Assembly of Odisha is unicameral, consisting of 147 Member of the Legislative Assembly (M.L.A). Its term is 5 years, unless sooner dissolved.

The state of Odisha is represented at the Centre by its 21 Member of Parliaments in the Lok Sabha and 10 Member of Parliaments in Rajya Sabha. There are 21 Lok Sabha constituencies from which candidates gets elected in the General Election to the Lok Sabha. The Members of Rajya Sabha were elected and / or nominated by the Member of Legislative Assembly through their parent political parties.

ODISHA LEGISLATIVE ASSEMBLY

The Odisha Legislative Assembly is the unicameral state legislature of Odisha state in eastern India. The seat of the Legislative Assembly is at Bhubaneshwar, the capital of the state. The Legislative Assembly comprises 147 Members of Legislative Assembly.

Procedure

Sessions and Time of Sittings

The Governor from time to time summons the Assembly to meet at such time and place as thinks fit, but the gap between the Assembly's last sitting in one session and the date appointed for its first sitting in the next session cannot exceed 6 months. The Governor may also from time to time prorogue the Assembly or dissolve the Assembly.

When the Governor summons the Assembly, summons are sent to each member by name, indicating the date, time and place appointed by the Governor for the session of the Assembly.

Prorogation by the Governor terminates the session of the Assembly and within a session the Speaker may adjourn the House from time to time or adjourn sine die.

Subject to Article 174 of the Constitution of India read with rule 11 of Rules of Procedure and Conduct of Business in the Orissa Legislative Assembly, in every calendar year the Assembly is required to have minimum of three sessions with minimum 60 sittings days

Unless the Speaker otherwise desires, the sitting of the Assembly commences at 10:30 am local time and concludes at 7 pm local time with a lunch break of two hours which is from 1 pm to 3 pm local time.

Under special circumstance, the speaker can allow the House to continue till 9 pm local time.

Procedure

All items of businesses require a notice period as follows:-

Questions - 14 clear days (Rule37)

Resolutions - 15 clear days (Rule-98-B)

Amendments to resolutions – 3 clear days (Rule 103)

Private Members' Bills - 30 clear days (Rule 66)

Amendment to Bills - 2 clear days (Rule 81)

Motions - 15 days (Rule 111)

Motions for reduction of demands, i.e.Cut-Motions - 5 days (Rule 124)

Half-an-hour discussion - 3 days (Rule 57)

Resolution for removal of Speaker -14 days (Article 179)

Adjournment Motion - One hour before the sitting (Rule 59)

Question Hour

For the purpose of answering questions, the Departments of Government are divided into groups and dates are fixed for each group. The Ministers concerned are required to answer the questions relating to the group.

The first hour of every sitting of the Assembly is available for answering questions. Questions are classified as

- Starred Questions
- Unstarred Questions
- Short Notice Starred Questions.

If a member desires oral answer, he is required to indicate the question by putting an asterisk mark (*) before it. The questions are answered in the order in which they are printed in the list of questions put for the day. Members are restricted to three such questions for any sitting day. The questions are asked in the order listed by the member who requested it. Supplementary questions can be asked for the purpose of eliciting further information on any matter of fact. The Speaker decides the number of supplementary questions according to the importance of a question.

On urgent matter and matters of public importance, members are allowed to put short notice questions, in which case notice period of 14 clear days is not observed. The speaker has the discretion of allowing such a question and the time period for a response from the ministry involved. If the Minister is unable to answer, the question is disallowed but if the Speaker is of the opinion that the question is of sufficient public importance, he may direct that it be answered as the first question on the day allotted to the group.

Notices of questions are required to be in writing in appropriate forms. In order that a question may be admissible, it is required to satisfy the various conditions detailed in the Rules of Procedure and Conduct of Business in the House. The Speaker decides the admissibility of questions. After a question is admitted, it is sent to the department concerned for furnishing answers to the Minister concerned.

List of Starred, Unstarred and Short Notice question are drawn for each category and circulated to all concerned. Questions are listed as per the order of priority determined by ballot. The dates on which ballot will be held are intimated to members sufficiently in advance. Members are free to witness the ballot.

Any member is allowed to give notice to raise a half-an-hour discussion on matter of sufficient public importance which has been the subject of a question, oral or written and the answers need elucidation on matter of fact. The Speaker may allot half-an-hour on three sittings in a week for such discussion.

Main Business

The main business of the day may be consideration of a Bill or financial business or consideration of a resolution or a motion.

A bill is a draft of an Act introduced in the Legislature by the Minister. It consists of (1) the title, (2) the enacting formula, (3) the body of the Bill which is divided into clauses with the statement of objects and reasons

Introduction of Bill

The Speaker may order the publication of any Bill (together with the statement of objects and reasons accompanying) in the Gazette, although no motion has been made for leave to introduce the Bill. In that case, it is not necessary to move for leave to introduce the Bill and if the Bill in afterwards introduced, it is necessary to publish it again. The Speaker will cause a copy of the notice and of the Bill together with the statement of objects and reasons to be forwarded to the Secretary to the Governor and the Law Department.

Whenever a Bill seeking to replace and ordinance with or without modification is introduced in the House, it is placed before the House along with the Bill, a statement explaining the circumstances which had necessitated immediate legislation by ordinance. Whenever an ordinance, which embodies wholly or partly or with modification the provisions of a Bill pending before the House, is promulgated a statement explaining the circumstances, which had necessitated immediate legislation by ordinance is laid on the Table during the Session following the promulgation of the ordinance.

If a motion for leave to introduce a Bill is opposed the Speaker after permitting, if he thinks fit, a brief explanatory statement from the member who opposes and from the member who moves the motion may, without further debate, put the question thereon. As soon as may be after a Bill has been introduced, the Bill unless it has already been published, is published in the Gazette.

Any member is allowed to ask for any paper or return connected with any Bill before the Assembly. The Speaker has the power to determine, either at the time or at the meeting of the Assembly next following whether the papers or returns asked for can be given.

Motions after introduction of a bill

When a bill is introduced or on some subsequent occasion, the Member-in-Charge may make one of the following motions in regard to his bill, namely: (i) that it be taken into consideration; or (ii) that it be referred to a Select Committee composed of such members of the Assembly and with instruction, if any, to report before such date as may be specified in the motion; or (iii) that it be circulated for the purpose of eliciting opinion thereon by a date to be specified in the motion:

Provided that no such motion shall be made until after copies of the bill have been made available for the use of members and that any member may object to any such motion being made unless copies of the Bill have been so made available for seven days before the day on which the motion is made and such objection shall prevail unless the Speaker allows the motion to be made.

On the date on which any motion referred to in Rule 70 is made or on any subsequent date to which discussion thereof is postponed, the principle of the Bill and its provision may be discussed generally, but the details of the Bill shall not be discussed further than is necessary to explain its principles.

At this stage no amendments to the Bill may be moved, but-

(a) If the Member-in-Charge moves that the Bill be taken into consideration, any member may move as an amendment that the Bill be referred to a Select Committee, or be circulated for the purpose of eliciting opinion thereon by a date to be specified in the motion.

(b) If the Member-in-Charge moves that the Bill be referred to a Select Committee, any member may move as an amendment that the Bill be circulated for the purpose of eliciting opinion thereon by a date to be specified in the motion.

Where a motion that a Bill be circulated for the purpose of eliciting opinion thereon is carried and the Bill is circulated in accordance with that direction and opinions are received thereon, the Member-in-Charge if he wishes to proceed with the Bill thereafter, shall move that the Bill be referred to a Select Committee unless the Speaker allows a motion to be made that the Bill be taken into consideration.

No motion that the Bill be taken into consideration or be passed shall be made by any member other than the Member-in-Charge of Bill and no motion that a Bill be referred to a Select Committee or be circulated for the purpose of eliciting opinion thereon shall be made by any member other than the Member-in-Charge except by way of amendment to a motion made

With regard to reference of the Bill to Select Committee and the procedure adopted thereon are laid down under the Rule 73 to 80 of the Rules of Procedure and Conduct of Business in the Orissa Legislative Assembly.

Amendments to clauses, etc. and consideration of Bill

If notice of an amendment has not been given two days before the day on which the Bill is to be considered any member may object to the moving of the amendment and such objection shall prevail unless the Speaker allows the amendment to be moved : Provided that in the case of Government Bill, an amendment of which notice has been received from the Member-in-Charge has ceased to be a Minister or a Member and such amendment shall stand in the name of the new Member-in-Charge of the Bill. (2) The Secretary shall, if time permits make available to members from time to time lists of amendments of which notices have been received. Conditions of admissibility of amendments are detailed under Rules 82 of the Rules of Procedure and Conduct of Business in the Orissa Legislative Assembly.

Amendments shall ordinarily be considered in the order of the clauses of the bill to which they respectively relate. An amendment moved may by leave of the Assembly but not otherwise be withdrawn on the request of the member moving it. If an amendment has been proposed to an amendment, the original amendment shall not be withdrawn until the amendment proposed to it has been disposed of.

Passing of Bill

When a motion that a Bill be taken into consideration has been carried and no amendment of the Bill is made, the Member-in-Charge may at once move that the Bill be passed. If any amendment of the Bill is made, any member may object to any motion being made on the same day that the Bill be passed and such objection shall prevail unless the Speaker allows the motion to be made. Where the objection prevails, a motion that the Bill be passed may be brought forward on any future day. No amendments, not being merely verbal shall be made to any Bill after such a motion is moved.

The discussion on a motion that the Bill be passed shall be confined to the submission of arguments either in support of the Bill or for the rejection of the Bill without going into it details. When a Bill which has been passed by the Assembly is returned by the Governor for reconsideration, the point or points referred for reconsideration shall be put before the Assembly by the Speaker and shall be discussed and voted upon in the same manner as amendments to a Bill, or in such other way as the Speaker may consider most convenient for their consideration by the Assembly.

Adjournment of Debate and Withdrawal and Removal of Bill

At any stage of a Bill which is under discussion in the Assembly, a motion that the debate on the Bill be adjourned may be moved with consent of the Speaker.

The Member who has introduced a Bill may at any stage of the Bill move that the Bill be withdrawn Provided that where a Bill has been referred to a Select Committee, notice of any motion for the withdrawal of the Bill shall automatically stand referred to the committee and after the Committee has expressed its opinion in a report to the Assembly the motion shall be set down in the list of business.

If a motion for leave to withdraw a Bill is opposed the Speaker may, if he thinks fit permit the Member who moves and the Members who opposes the motion to make brief explanatory statements and may thereafter, without further debate, put the question.

Procedure regarding Non-Official Bills

Members may give notice of Bills. In the first instance the Members should give 30 days notice of their intention to move for leave to introduce a Bill and send a copy of the Bill together with a statement of objects and reasons.

An intimation will be sent to the concerned Member if the Bill requires the recommendation of the Governor for introduction or for its consideration. It is the responsibility of the Member-in-Charge to obtain Governor's recommendation and annex to the notice.

On the day on which the item is included in the agenda, the Member concerned should move for leave to introduce the Bill and after the leave is granted formally to introduce the Bill. The Bill after introduction, will be published in the Gazette. If the Bill does not require the recommendation of the Governor for its consideration, the Member concerned should give notice of his intention to move for consideration of the Bill and for the Bill being passed.

Governor's (or President's) Assent to Bill

Assent is the final stage in the making of a law. It is the Act where by the Governor (or President, if a Bill is reserved for his assent) gives his assent to the Bill passed by House after which it is published as an Act of the Legislature.

Amendments

An amendment is an alternation proposed or made in a motion. It must be either to insert certain words in the motion or Bill or to leave out certain words or substitute others. Notice of amendments should be in writing, signed and given to the office before the time prescribed for its receipt. Members, who give amendments should clearly indicate to which clause or sub-clause of a Bill their amendments relate. Amendments received in the office after the prescribed time are liable to be rejected. No notice of amendment need to be given for deleting a whole clause in a Bill. Members who want the deletion of a whole clause may oppose the clause itself when it is put to vote.

Financial Business

Copies of the Budget papers including Supplementary Budget and Excess Demand are supplied to Members soon after the same is presented.

The Budget is disposed of a in two stages, i.e. general discussion and voting on demands, Members may participate in the general discussion and speak on the Budget as a whole or any question of principle involved therein, but no motion shall be moved at this stage. In the case of Supplementary Budget, Excess Demand, etc. no general discussion takes place.

A Member may give notice of Motions for reduction of Demands (Cut Motion) in the prescribed form available in the office. On the recommendation of the Business Advisory Committee, a time table showing the dates on which demands will be taken up for voting and the dates of giving notice of Cut Motion is circulated. Cut Motions received after the prescribed date and time are rejected.

On the last day of the days allotted for voting on demands at 17.00 Hrs. or at such other hour as the Speaker may fix, the Speaker shall forthwith put every question necessary to dispose of all outstanding matters in connection with the demands for grants, which process is called the "Guillotine'.

Motions for reduction of Demands for Grants :

(1) Cut-motions are divided into the following three categories—

    (i) Refusal of supplies, i.e., a motion to reduce the amount of demand to a nominal figure of one rupee. Such motions are intended to refuse supplies because the whole policy underlying this demand is disapproved by a member. Under each demand motions of this category are arranged in the "List of Motions" in the order of receipt. In the case of such motions, no question proposed to be raised need be indicated in brackets except the words refusal of supplies. If any specific grievance is indicated therein the motion will be treated as a "Token Cut " for determining priority.

    (ii) Economy cut, i.e. a Cut-motion for the purpose of effecting economy or retrenchment in the "List of Motions". Such motions are entered under the relevant Demand after the motions for Refusal of supplies are arranged in the List of Motions according to the amounts of the cuts proposed. In this case there is no need to mention any specific grievance. The word "economy" should be mentioned and an indication may be given of the particular sub-head or item in respect of which retrenchment of economy is proposed.

(2) The "List of Motions" under the various demands for grants is arranged as explained above. But before the Demands for grants are actually discussed in the Assembly on the days allotted for this purpose the demands that should be discussed are selected by the Business Advisory Committee.

(iii) Token Cut, i.e., a Cut-Motion for a nominal figure in order to ventilate a specific grievance. In giving notices of such motions it is the established practice for members to indicate briefly within brackets the question which they want to raise on each motion for reduction separately. Only one grievance can be discussed on each such uniform figure of cut viz. Rs. 100. These motions are entered after the economy cuts and are arranged in the list of motion in the order of receipt irrespective of amount of the cut. In moving such motions, suggestions to amend existing legislation are not in order. Moreover, a special demand is put down to cover a specific and particular subject, it can be discussed only under that specific demand and not under any other demand.

Since the Demands which the Finance Minister may subsequently find necessary to present to the Assembly for excess grant and for supplementary or additional grants are dealt the same manner by the Assembly as if they were demands for grants. It is open to members to give notice of Cut-Motions in respect of such demands also.

POLITICS OF ODISHA

Politics in Odisha takes place within a framework of a federal parliamentary representative democratic republic, where the Union Government of India exercises sovereign rights with certain powers reserved to the states of India including Odisha. The state has a multi-party system where the two main parties are the centrist and secularist Indian National Congress (INC) and the regional socialistparty Biju Janata Dal (BJD). The nationalist Bharatiya Janata Party (BJP) has increased in recent years. The Governor of Odisha is appointed by the Union Government and can, in some circumstances, dismiss the state government.

4

Language and Literature

LANGUAGES OF ODISHA (ORISSA)

A direct descendant of eastern Magadhi, Oriya is the principal and regional language of Odisha (Orissa). Belonging to the Aryan family of languages, it is closely related to Assamese, Bengali and Maithili. Under the influence of neighboring regional languages of the Aryan and Dravidian families, Oriya has developed many linguistic variations, such as Baleswari (Balasore), Bhatri (Koraput), Laria (Sambalpur), Sambalpuri (Sambalpur and other western districts), Ganjami (Ganjam and Koraput), Chhatisgarhi (Chhatisgarh and adjoining areas of Odisha (Orissa)) and Medinipuri (Midnapur district of West Bengal).

Besides, hilly regions of north and south Odisha (Orissa) have their own local versions of Oriya with many linguistic peculiarities. The first dated, inscription in Oriya goes back to 1051 AD discovered at Urajang. But some of the recent discoveries of Sanskrit inscriptions with Oriya words reported from certain areas of the ancient Kalinga Empire push back its lineage to the 6th century AD.

The Oriya script, descending from Brahmi, has been given Dravidian finish, probably during the reign of the Ganga kings.

And the shape was admirably adapted to writing on processed palm leaves with an iron stylus.

ODIA LITERATURE

Odia language literature is the predominant literature of the state of Odisha in India. The language is also spoken by minority populations of the neighbouring states of Jharkhand, West Bengal, Chhattisgarh and Andhra Pradesh. The region has been known at different stages of history as Kalinga, Udra, Utkala or Hirakhanda. Odisha was a vast empire in ancient and medieval times, extending from the Ganges in the north to the Godavari in the south. During British rule, however, Odisha lost its political identity and formed parts of the Bengal and Madras Presidencies. The present state of Odisha was formed in 1936. The modern Odia language is formed mostly from Pali words with significant Sanskrit influence. About 28% of modern Odia words have Adivasi origins, and about 2% have Hindustani (Hindi/Urdu), Persian, or Arabic origins. The earliest written texts in the language are about thousand years old.The first Odia newspaper was Utkala Deepika first published on 4 August 1866.

Odia is the only Indo-European language of India other than Sanskrit and the sixth Indian language that has been conferred classical language status and forms the basis of Odissi dance and Odissi music.

Historians have divided the history of the Odia language literature into five main stages: Old Odia (8th century to 1300), Early Middle Odia (1300 to 1500), Middle Odia (1500 to 1700), Late Middle Odia (1700 to 1850) and Modern Odia (1850 to present). Further subdivisions, as seen below, can more accurately chart the language's development.

First Literature of Odisha (4th centuries BC)

The ancientness of the Odia literature is being proved from its soil which says about two types of literature from very beginning. The development of Odia can be seen through its spoken and written forms. The spoken literature are expressed two ways. One preserved through folk forms and the other preserved through inscriptions. The songs sungs at the time of birth, death and work conditions are preserved, stories are painted through cave paintings both represent the creativity of the underlying literature. The inhabitant of this land stated to drown this language at about fifteen thousand years back. The Gudahandi painting of Kalahandi district and the cave art of Khandagiri and Udayagiri are the great achievements of this primitive architecture.

Kharavel's Hatigumpha inscription is the real evidence of past Odia cultural, political, ritual and social status and it is the 1st poetic stake inscription. Though Ashok has created many rock edicts and inscription before Kharavela, yet his instructions for administration have been written in a rude and chocked language. On the other hand, the Hatigumpha inscriptionshow the flexibility of a language in a sweet flow.

Main feature of this inscription was based on principles of Sanskrit poetic structure: such as-

Sadvanshah kshyatriya bâ pi dhiirodâttah gunanwitâh I
Ekabanshodva bhupâhâ kulajâ bahabo pi Jâ II
Shrungarabirashantânâmekoangirasa ishyate I
Angâni sarbe<pi rasâha sarbe nâtakasandhyâhâ II
Itihâsodvabam bruttamânânyad bâ sajjanâshrayam I
Chatwarastasya bargahâ syusteshwekam cha phalam bhavet II
Aâdyu namaskriyashribâ bastunirddesha eba bâ I
Kwacinnindâ khalâdinâm satâm cha gunakirttinam II
(Sâhitya darpan- Biswanâth kabirâj)

It means that such creations will be called as poem which Protagonist would be Dhirodatta belonging to an untouchable kshtriya. In Rasa (aesthetics) Srunagâra (Love, Attractiveness), Vîra (Heroic mood), Sânta (Peace or tranquility)among them one would be tha main rasa and others are remain with them as usual. All aspects of drama, historic tales and other legendary folklores are present. The description of all the four fold-Dharma, Artha, Kama and Mokshya are still present here, but one should be given priority than other theme. At the beginning it should be written as respective, blissful and subject aware with welfare of people being hatred towards evil and devotional towards sages/saints.

When Hatigumpha Inscription was created by Kharavela, all these principles were traced by him before, which has been followed by Rudradaman (Girinar inscription-150 A.D.), Samudragupta (Prayaga inscription-365 A.D), Kumargupta (Mandasore inscription-473A.D.) etc, created their own famous creativities in a decent poetic style on many rocks in Sanskrit language. The trend of writing was not obstructed after Kharavela. From Asanapata inscription in Keonjhar created by Satru Bhanja, (a warrior of Odisha)were engraved in the temple, Laxminarayana of Simhanchalam by Mukunda Deva are such examples. At the beginning, these inscriptions had a dynamic journy from Pali to Sanskrit. They have not lost the sense of Odia. Therefore, Odia language, literature, script and culture are based on the discussions on these inscriptions. The words written in the Hatigumpha Inscription is still used in the present day Odia language.

Age of Charya literature (7th – 8th centuries AD)

The beginnings of Odia poetry coincide with the development of Charyapada or Caryagiti, a literature started by Vajrayana Buddhist poets. This literature was written with a certain metaphor called "Sandhya Bhasha", and some of its poets like Luipa and Kanhupa came from the territory of Odisha. The language of Charya was considered to be Prakrit. In one of his poem, Kanhupa wrote:

Your hut stands outside the city

Oh, untouchable maid

The bald Brahmin passes sneaking close by

Oh, my maid, I would make you my companion

Kanha is a kapali, a yogi

He is naked and has no disgust

There is a lotus with sixty-four petals

Upon that the maid will climb with this poor self and dance.

In this poem shakti is replaced by the image of the "untouchable maid". The description of its location outside the city corresponds to being outside the ordinary consciousness. Although she is untouchable the bald Brahmin, or in other words so-called wise man, has a secret hankering for her. But only a *kapali* or an extreme tantric can be a fit companion for her, because he is also an outcast. The kapali is naked because he does not have any social identity or artifice. After the union with the shakti, the shakti and the kapali will climb on the 64-petalled lotus Sahasrara chakra and dance there.

This poet used images and symbols from the existing social milieu or collective psychology so that the idea of a deep realization could be easily grasped by the readers. This kind of poetry, full of the mystery of tantra, spread throughout the northeastern part of India from the 10th to the 14th century, and its style of expression was revived by the Odia poets of the 16th to the 19th century.

Pre-Sarala Age (12th – 14th century AD)

In the pre-Sarala period, Natha and Siddha literature flourished in Odisha. The main works of this period are *Shishu veda* (an anthology of 24 dohas), *Amara Kosha* and *Gorakha Samhita*. *Shishu veda* is mentioned in the works of Sarala Das and the later 16th century poets. It is written in Dandi brutta. Raja Balabhadra Bhanja wrote the love story, *Bhagabati* known for its emotional content. The other important works of this period are the *Kalasha Chautisha* (By Baccha Das), *Somanatha bratakatha, Nagala chauthi, Tapoi* and *Saptanga*.

Rudrasudhanidhi is considered the first work of prose in Odia literature written by Abhadutta Narayan Swami.

Markanda Das composed the first Koili (an ode to cuckoo) in Odia just before the beginning of the age of Sarala Das. His composition *Kesava Koili* describes the pain of separation of Yasoda from her son Krishna. He is also known to compose the epic *Daasagriba badha, Jnaanodaya koili* etc.

Age of Sarala Dasa

In the 15th century, Sanskrit was the lingua franca for literature in Odisha and Odia was often considered the language of the commoners and shudras (Untouchables), who had no access to Sanskrit education. The first great poet of Odisha with widespread readership is the famous Sarala-Das, who translated the *Mahabharata*. This was not an exact translation from the Sanskrit original, but rather an imitation; for all practical purposes it can be seen as an original piece of work. Sarala Dasa was given the title Shudramuni, or seer from a backward class. He had no formal education and did not know Sanskrit.

This translation has since provided subsequent poets with the necessary foundation for a national literature, providing a fairly accurate idea of the Odia culture at the time. Sarala Dasa, born in the 15th century Odisha of the Gajapati emperor Kapilendra Deva, was acclaimed as the "Adikabi" or first poet. The reign of the Gajapatis is considered the golden period for Odisha's art and literature. Kapilendra Deva patronized Odia language and literature along with Sanskrit unlike his predecessors who used only Sanskrit as their lingua franca. In fact a short Odia poem *Kebana Munikumara* is found in the Sanskrit Drama *Parashurama Vijaya* ascribed to none other than the emperor Kapilendra Deva himself. It is believed that Sarala Dasa's poetic gift came from the goddess Sarala (Saraswati), and that Sarala-Dasa wrote the Mahabharata as she dictated it. Though he wrote many poems and epics, he is best remembered for the *Mahabharata*. His other most known works are *Chandi Purana* and the *Vilanka Ramayana*. He also composed the *Lakshmi-Narayana Bachanika*.

Arjuna Dasa, a contemporary of Sarala-Das, wrote *Rama-Bibha*, which is a significant long poem in Odia. He is also the author of another kavya called *Kalpalata*.

Age of the Panchasakhas

Five Odia poets emerged during the late 15th and early 16th centuries: Balaram Das, Atibadi Jagannath Das, Achyutananda Das, Ananta Das and Jasobanta Das. Although they wrote over a span of one hundred years they are collectively known as the "Panchasakhas", since they adhered to the same school of thought, Utkaliya Vaishnavism. The word "pancha" means five and the word "sakha", friend.

The Panchasakhas are Vaishnavas by thought. In 1509, Chaitanya came to Odisha with his Vaishnava message of love. Before him, Jaydev had prepared the ground for Vaishnavism through his Gita Govinda. Chaitanya's path of devotion was known as Raganuga Bhakti Marga. He introduced chanting as a way to make spiritual connection & taught the importance of Hare krushna mantra. Unlike Chaitanya, the Panchasakhas believed in Gyana Mishra Bhakti Marga, similar to the Buddhist philosophy of Charya literature stated above.

The Panchasakhas were significant not only because of their poetry but also for their spiritual legacy. In the holy land of Kalinga (Odisha) several saints, mystics, and devotional souls have been born throughout history, fortifying its culture and spiritualism. The area uniquely includes temples of Shakti, Shiva and Jagannâtha Vishnu. Several rituals and traditions have been extensively practised here by various seers - including Buddhist ceremonies, Devi "Tantra" (tantric rituals for Shakti), Shaiva Marg and Vaishnava Marg. There is hardly any "Sadhak" who did not pay a visit to the Shri Jagannâth temple.

There is an interesting description of the origin of the Panchasakhas, in Achyutananda's *Shunya Samhita*. As per his narration, towards the end of Mahabharat when Lord Krishna was leaving his mortal body, Nilakantheswara Mahadeva appeared & revealed to him that the Lord's companions Dama, Sudama, Srivatsa, Subala, and Subahu would reincarnate in the Kali-yuga & be known as Ananta, Acyutananda, Jagannatha, Balarama and Yasovanta, respectively. Thus, believers in the Panchasakha consider them the most intimate friends of Lord Krishna in Dwapara-yuga, who came again in Kali-yuga to serve him. They are also instrumental in performing the crucial & much-awaited Yuga-Karma where they destroy the sinners and save the saints, according to Sanatana-Hindu beliefs.

Balaram Das's *Jagamohan Ramayan* provided one pillar, along with Sarala-Das's *Mahabharata*, upon which subsequent Odia literature was built. His *Laksmi Purana* is considered the first manifesto of women's liberation or feminism in Indian literature. His other major works are *Gita Abakasa, Bhava samudra, Gupta Gita, Vedanta Sara, Mriguni Stuti, Saptanga yogasara tika, Vedanta sara or Brahma tika, Baula gai gita, Kamala lochana chotisa, Kanta koili, Bedha parikrama, Brahma gita, Brahmanda bhugola, Vajra kavacha, Jnana chudamani, Virata gita, Ganesha vibhuti & Amarakosha Gita.*

The most influential work of this period was however Atibadi Jagannath Das's *Bhagabata*, which had a great influence on the Odia people as a day-to-day philosophical guide, as well as a lasting one in Odia culture. His other works include *Gupta Bhagavat, Tula vina, Sola chapadi, Chari chapadi, Tola bena, Daru brahma gita, Diksa samyad, Artha koili, Muguni stuti, Annamaya kundali, Goloka sarodhara, Bhakti chandrika, Kali malika, Indra malika, Niladri vilasa, Nitya gupta chintamani, Sri Krishna bhakti kalpa lata* etc.

Shishu Ananta Das was born in Balipatana near Bhubaneswar in the late 15th century. He wrote *Bhakti mukti daya gita, Sisu Deva gita, Artha tarani, Udebhakara, Tirabhakana,* a *Malika* and several bhajan poetries.

Yashobanta Das was the composer of *Govinda Chandra* (a ballad or Gatha- Sangeeta), *Premabhakti, Brahma Gita, Shiva Swarodaya, Sasti mala, Brahma gita, Atma pariche gita,* a *Malika* and several bhajans.

Mahapurusha Achyutananda is considered the most prolific writer of the Panchasakhas. He is believed to be born through special divine intervention from Lord Jagannath. The name Achyuta literally means "created from Lord Vishnu". He is also referred to as "Achyuti", i.e. "He who has no fall" in Odia. He was born to Dinabandhu Khuntia & Padma Devi in Tilakona, Nemal around 1485 AD. He established spiritual energetic centers called "gadis" all over east India (in the former states of Anga, Banga, Kalinga, Magadha) and Nepal. Gadis such as

Nemal, Kakatpur, Garoi, & Jobra Ghat were places for spiritual actions, discourses and penance. He was learned in Ayurveda, sciences & social regulations. His works are *Harivamsa, Tattva bodhini, Sunya samhita, Jyoti samhita, Gopala Ujjvala, Baranasi Gita, Anakara Brahma Samhita, Abhayada Kavacha, Astagujari, Sarana panjara stotra, Vipra chalaka, Manamahima, Maalika.*

The Panchasakha's individual characteristics are described as follows (in Odia and English):

Agamya bhâba jânee Yasovanta
Gâra katâ Yantra jânee Ananta
Âgata Nâgata Achyuta bhane
Balarâma Dâsa tatwa bakhâne
Bhaktira bhâba jâne Jagannâtha
Panchasakhaa e
mora pancha mahanta.
Yasovanta knows the things beyond reach
Yantras uses lines and figures known to Ananta
Achyuta speaks the past, present and future
Balarâma Dasa is fluent in tatwa (the ultimate meaning
of anything)
Ultimate feelings of devotion are known to Jagannâtha
These five friends are my five mahantas.

During the Panchasakha era another seer Raghu Arakhsita, who was not part of the Panchasakhas but was a revered saint, composed several Padabalis in Odia. The Panchasakha and Arakhshita together are known as the Sada-Goswami (six Lords).

Madhavi Pattanayak or Madhavi Dasi is considered as the first Odia woman poet who was a contemporary of Prataprudra Deva and wrote several devotional poetries for Lord Jagannatha.

Imaginative medieval Odia literature (16th – Mid 17th century)

Several Kaalpanika (imaginative) and Pauraanika (Puranic) Kavyas were composed during this period that formed the foundation for Riti Juga. The major works of this era other than those written by the Panchasakhas are *Gopakeli* and *Parimalaa* authored by Narasingha sena, contemporary of Gajapati emperor Prataprudra Deva, *Chataa Ichaamati* and *Rasa* by Banamali Das, *Premalochana, Bada Shakuntala & Kalaabati* by Vishnu Das, *Nrushingha purana* and *Nirguna Mahatmya* by Chaitanya Dash (born in Kalahandi), *Lilaabati* by Raghunatha Harichandan, *Usha Bilasa* by Shishu shankar Das, *Sasisena* by Pratap Rai, *Rahashya Manjari* by Devadurlava Das, *Hiraabati* by Ramachandra Chottaray, *Deulatola* by Nilambara Das, *Prema Panchamruta* by Bhupati Pandit, *Rukmini Vivaha* by Kartik Das, *Goparasa* by Danai Das and *Kanchi Kaveri* by Purushotama Das. In the 16th century three major poets translated Jayadeva's Gita Govinda into Odia. They are Dharanidhara Mishra, Brindavan Das(*Rasabaridhi*) and Trilochan Das (*GovindaGita*).Brundabati Dasi, a women poet of great talent wrote *Purnatama Chandrodaya Kavya* towards the end of seventeenth century.

Several Chautishas (a form of Odia poetry where 34 stanzas from "ka" to "Khsya" are placed at the starting of each composition) were composed during this time. The famous ones being *Milana Chautisha, Mandakini Chautisha, Barshabharana Chautisha, Rasakulya Chautisha* etc.

Muslim poet Salabega was one of the foremost devotional poets of this era who composed several poems dedicated to Lord Jagannath during Jahangir's reign in the 17th century.

Riti Yuga/Age of Upendra Bhanja (1650–1850)

After the age of the Panchasakhas, several prominent works were written, including the *Usabhilasa* of Sisu Sankara Das, the *Rahasya-manjari* of Deva-durlabha Dasa and the *Rukmini-bibha* of Karttika Das. A new form of novels in verse evolved at the beginning of the 17th century when Ramachandra Pattanayaka wrote *Haravali*. The prominent poets of the period, however, are Dhananjaya Bhanja (born 1611. AD), Dinakrushna Das (born 1650. AD), Kabi Samrat Upendra Bhanja (born 1670. AD) and Abhimanyu Samanta Simhar. Their poetry, especially that of

Upendra Bhanja, is characterised by verbal tricks, obscenity and eroticism.

Upendra Bhanja's works like *Baidehisha Bilasa, Koti Brahmanda Sundari* and *Labanyabati* are considered landmarks of Odia Literature. He was conferred with the title "Kabi Samrat" of Odia literature for his aesthetic poetic sense and skill with words. He wrote 52 books out of which only 25-26 are available. He alone contributed more than 35000 words to Odia literature and is considered the greatest poet of Riti Juga.

Dhananjaya Bhanja (1611-1701), a poet of repute, king of Ghumusar and grandfather of Upendra Bhanja, wrote several kavyas like *Anangarekha, Ichaavati, Raghunatha Bilasa, Madana Manjari* etc..

Besides Tribikrama Bhanja (author of *Kanakalata*) and Ghana Bhanja (author of *Trailokyamohini, Rasanidhi* and *Govinda Bilasha*) of the Bhanja royal family also enriched Odia Literature. Lokanatha Vidyadhara, a contemporary of Upendra Bhanja wrote *Sarbanga Sundari.*

Dinakrushna Das's *Rasokallola* and Abhimanyu Samanta Simhara's *Bidagdha Chintamani* are also prominent kavyas of this time. *Bidagdha Chintamani* is considered the longest Kavya in Odia literature with 96 cantos exceeding that of Upendra's longest kavya of 52 cantos. Other famous works of Abhimanyu Samanta Simhara are *Sulakhshyana, Prema Chintaamani, Prema Kala, Rasaabati, Prematarangini* etc. These poets significantly influenced modern Odia Literature.

A new form of poetry called *"Bandha kabita"* also started during this time where the poet wrote the poem within the bandha or frame of a picture drawn by him. Upendra Bhanja was the pioneer in this form of pictorial poetry. His Chitrakavya Bandhodaya is the first such creation containing 84 pictorial poems. Poets who wrote in this tradition include Sadananda Kabisurya Bramha (*Lalita Lochana* and *Prema Kalpalata*), Tribikrama Bhanja (*Kanakalata*), Kesabaraja Harichandana (*Rasa Sindhu Sulakhshyana*) etc.

Lyrical Odia Literature towards the end of Riti Juga:

Towards the end of Riti Yuga, four major poets emerged and enriched Odia literature through their highly lyrical creations. These were Kabi Surya Baladeb Rath, Brajanath Badajena, Gopal Krushna Pattanaik and Bhima Bhoi. Kabisurya Baladev Rath wrote his poems in champu (mixture of prose and poetry) and chautisha style of poetry. His greatest work is *Kishore Chandranana Champu* which is a landmark creation extensively used in Odissi Music. Brajanath Badjena started a tradition of prose fiction, though he was not an excellent prose writer. His *Chatur Binoda* (Amusement of Intelligent) seems to be the first work that deals with different kinds of rasas, predominantly the bibhatsa rasa, but often verges on nonsense. The style of *"Chitra Kavya"* (mixture of poetry and paintings) was at its best in the 18th century. Several chitra pothis can be traced to this time.

Bichitra Ramayana of Biswanaath Khuntia is one of the most celebrated works of this period composed in the early 18th century. Pitambar Das wrote the epic *Narasingha Purana*consisting of seven parts called *Ratnakaras* in the 18th century. Maguni Pattanaik composed the *Rama Chandra Vihara*. *Rama Lila* was composed by Vaishya Sadashiva and Ananga Narendra. Bhima Bhoi, the blind poet born in a tribal Khondh family is known for his lucid and humanistic compositions like *Stuthi Chintaamani, Bramha Nirupana Gita, Shrutinishedha Gita* etc.The other major poets towards the end of Riti Yuga are Banamali, Jadumani Mohapatra, Bhaktacharan Das (author of *Manabodha Chautisha* and *Mathura Mangala*), Haribandhu, Gaurahari, Gauracharana, Krishna Simha all of whom enriched Odia lyrical literature.

Age of Radhanath

The first printing of the Odia language was done in 1836 by Christian missionaries, replacing palm leaf inscription and revolutionising Odia literature. After this time books were printed and journals and periodicals became available in Odia. The first Odia magazine, *Bodha Dayini* was published in Balasore in 1861. Its goal was to promote Odia literature and draw attention to lapses in government policy. The first Odia paper *The Utkala Deepika*, was first published in 1866 under editor Gourishankar Ray and Bichitrananda. *The Utkal Deepika* campaigned to bring all Odia-speaking areas together under one administration, to develop the Odia language and literature and to protect Odia interests.

In 1869 Bhagavati Charan Das started another newspaper, *Utkal Subhakari*, to propagate the Brahmo faith. In the last three and a half decades of the 19th century, a number of newspapers were published in Odia. Prominent papers included *Utkal Deepika, Utkal Patra, Utkal Hiteisini* from Cuttack, *Utkal Darpan* and *Sambada Vahika* from Balasore and *Sambalpur Hiteisini* from Deogarh. The success of these papers indicated the desire and determination of the people of Odisha to uphold their right to freedom of expression and freedom of the press, with the ultimate aim of freedom from British rule. These periodicals performed another vital function, in that they encouraged modern literature and offered a broad reading base for Odia-language writers. Intellectuals who came into contact with Odia literature through the papers were also influenced by their availability.

Radhanath Ray (1849–1908) is the most well-known poet of this period. He wrote with a Western influence, and his kavyas (long poems) included Chandrabhaga, Nandikeshwari, Usha, Mahajatra, Darbar and Chilika.

Fakir Mohan Senapati (1843–1918), the most known Odia fiction writer, was also of this generation. He was considered the Vyasakabi or founding poet of the Odia language. Senapati was born raised in the coastal town of Balasore, and worked as a government administrator. Enraged by the attempts of the Bengalis to marginalize or replace the Odia language, he took to creative writing late in life. Though he also did translations from Sanskrit, wrote poetry and attempted many forms of literature, he is now known primarily as the father of modern Odia prose fiction. His *Rebati* (1898) is widely recognized as the first Odia short story. *Rebati* is the story of a young innocent girl whose desire for education is placed in the context of a conservative society in a backward Odisha village, which is hit by the killer cholera epidemic. His other stories are "Patent Medicine", "Dak Munshi", and "Adharma Bitta". Senapati is also known for his novel Chha Maana Atha Guntha. This was the first Indian novel to deal with the exploitation of landless peasants by a feudal lord. It was written well before the October revolution in Russia and emerging of Marxist ideas in India.

Other eminent Odia writers and poets of the time include Gangadhar Meher (1862–1924), Madhusudan Rao, Chintamani Mohanty, Nanda Kishore Bal and Gaurisankar Ray.

Age of Satyabadi

During the Age of Radhanath the literary world was divided between the classicists, led by the magazine *The Indradhanu*, and the modernists, led by the magazine *The Bijuli*. Gopabandhu Das (1877–1928) was a great balancer and realized that a nation, as well as its literature, lives by its traditions. He believed that a modern national superstructure could only endure if based on solid historical foundations. He wrote a satirical poem in *The Indradhanu*, which led to punishment by the Inspector of Schools, but he refused to apologise.

Gopabandhu joined Ravenshaw College in Cuttack to pursue graduation after this incident. He started the *Kartavya Bodhini Samiti* (Duty Awakening Society) in college to encourage his friends to take on social, economic and political problems and become responsible citizens. While leading a team to serve flood victims, Gopabandhu heard that his son was seriously ill. He preferred, however, to save the "sons of the soil" rather than his son. His mission was to reform society and develop education in the name of a social service vision. He lost his wife at age twenty-eight, and had already lost all three of his sons by this time. He left his two daughters and his property in the village with his elder brother, rejecting worldly life. For this social service mission he is regarded by Odias as the Utkalmani.

As freedom movements began, a new era in literary thought emerged influenced by Gandhi and the trend of nationalism. Gopabandhu was a large part of this idealistic movement, founding a school in Satyabadi and influencing many writers of the period. Other than Gopabandhu himself, other famous writers of the era were Godabarisha Mishra, Nilakantha Dash, Harihara Acharya and Krupasinshu. They are known as 'Panchasakhas' for their similarities with the historical Age of Panchasakhas. Their principle genres were criticism, essays and poetry.

Chintamani Das is particularly renowned. Born in 1903 in Sriramachandrapur village near Sakhigopal, he was bestowed with the Sahitya Akademi Samman in 1970 for his invaluable contribution to Odia literature. Some of his well-known literary works are *Manishi Nilakantha, Bhala Manisa Hua, Usha, Barabati, Byasakabi Fakiramohan* and *Kabi Godabarisha*.

Pragati Yuga

Nabajuga Sahitya Sansad formed in 1935 was one of the first progressive literary organizations in India. It was formed before the National Progressive Writers Association was established in 1936 by Munshi Prem Chand, Sajad Zaheer, Mulk Raj Anand and others. The founders of the Progressive Movement in Orissa were Nabakrushna Choudhury, Bhagabati Panigrahi and Ananta Patnaik. At the inaugural session of Nabajuga Sahitya Sansad, the great freedom fighter Malati Choudhury sang "Nabeena Jugara Taruna Jagare" written by Ananta Patnaik. The mouth piece of Nabajuga Sahity Sansad was Adhunika, the First Progressive Literary Magazine in Oriya. Adhuinka was conceived, initiated, edited, published and nurtured by Bhagabati Charan Panigrahi and Ananta Patnaik. Many writers of that time wrote in Adhunika.

Age of Romanticism or Sabuja Yuga

Influenced by the Romantic thoughts of Rabindranath Tagore during the 1930s when progressive Marxist movements dominated Odia Literature, Kalindi Charan Panigrahi (the brother of Bhagabati Charan Panigrahi who founded Marxism in Odisha) formed a group called "Sabuja Samiti" with two of his writer friends Annada Shankar Ray and Baikuntha Patnaik.

This was a very short period in Odia literature, later folded into Gandhian and Marxist work. Kalindi Charan Panigrahi later wrote his famous novel *Matira Manisha*, which was influenced by Gandhism, and Annada Shankar Ray left for Bengali literature. Mayadhar Mansingh was a renowned poet of that time, but though he was considered a Romantic poet he kept his distance from the influence of Rabindranath.

Purnachandra Odia Bhashakosha

The *Purnachandra Odia Bhashakosha* is a monumental 7-volume work of about 9,500 pages published between 1930 and 1940. It was a result of the vision and dedicated work of Gopal Chandra Praharaj (1874–1945) over nearly three decades. Praharaj not only conceived of and compiled the work, he also raised the finances to print it through public donations, grants and subscriptions and supervised the printing and the sales of the published work.

The Purnachandra Odia Bhashakosha is an Odia language dictionary that lists some 185,000 words and their meanings in four languages - Odia, English, Hindi and Bengali. It includes quotations from wide-ranging classical works illustrating the special usage of various words.

It also contains specialised information such as botanical names of local plants, information on astronomy and long articles on various topics of local interest. In addition, there are biographies of personalities connected with Odisha's history and culture.

The Purnachandra Odia Bhashakosha is an encyclopaedic work touching on various aspects of the Odia language and Odisha region, as well as many topics of general interest. Its author Praharaj was a lawyer by profession and was ridiculed and reviled by many during production itself. Many printed copies were destroyed unbound and unsold. Many copies sat in libraries of the princes who had patronised the work and most of these copies were sold cheaply when the princes met financial ruin. There are few surviving copies, and those that exist are fragile and worm-damaged. The work is regarded by the older generation, but not well-known among younger Odias.

Post Colonial Age

Poetry

As the successors of Sachi Routray, the father of modern poetry, two poets (Guruprasad Mohanty and Bhanuji Rao) were highly influenced by T.S. Eliot and published a co-authored poetry book *Nutan Kabita*. Ramakanta Rath later modified Eliot's ideas in his own work. According to Rath : "After the publication of Kalapurusha [Guru Prasad's poetry collection influenced by T.S. Eliot's *The Waste Land*] we realized that a sense of alienation is the main ingredient of modern poetry." Before independence Odia poetry was mostly written with Sanskritic or "literary" idiom, but after independence poets freely used of Western concepts, idioms, images and adaptation of Western myths.Ramakanta Rath, Sitakant Mahapatra, Soubhagya Kumar Mishra, Rajendra kishore Panda, Prativa Satpathy, Mamata Dash, Haraprasad Das are the most famous of these poets. The mid 60s and between 70s the prominent poets of Odia were- Radhamohan Gadnayak, Benudhar Rout, Brajanath Rath, Bangali Nanda, Harihar Mishra, Dipak Mishra, Kamalakant Lenka, Banshidhar Sarangi, Durga Charan Parida, Devdas Chhotray, Saroj Ranjan Mohanty, Amaresh Patnaik, Ashutosh Parida, Prasanna Patsani, Hussain Rabi Gandhi, Sadasiba Dash, Goutam Jena, one of the wide circulated odia poet.He is born on 7th.May1959.He is the pioneer of"Groundism", that is"Matimanaskabad".His poem collections are "samaya BISADA nai","Ekaeka Dina", Ranga Siuli", MayaManaska", Panchama Raga", Bahuda Bela", Jibana Veda"and Darsana Yoga. Hrishkesh Mullick, Satrughna Pandab, Prabasini Mahakuda, Aaparna Mohanty, Aswini Mishra, Roninikant Mukherjee, Girija Baliarsingh etc. The early 80s saw in Odia Literature a Group of poets with new thoughts and style who overshadowed the earlier generation. These poets had their root in typical Odia soil. The rich heritage and culture with the feelings of commomen were depicted in their Odia poems. They were somehow more nearer to the readers as there were little ambiguity in their expression These contemporary poems were better than the so-called modern poems. The prominent poets of this time were- Manasi Pradhan, Surya Mishra, Bhagirathi Mishra, Ramakrushna Sahoo, Abani Pradhan, Bijay Mahapatra, Kanhu Charan Panigrahi, Manas Ranjan Mohapatra, Akshaya Behera, Samarendranath Mahapatra, Sunil Prusty, Chittaranjan Misra, Senapati Pradyumna Keshari, Ajay Pradhan, Sucheta Mishra, Manoranjan Panigrahi, Raxak Nayak, Arupananda Panigrahi, Biraja Bala, Khirod Parida, Ranjan Kumar Das, Akhila Nayak, Pabitra Mohan Dash, Kedar Mishra, Basudev Sunani, Lenin Kumar, Dr. Basanta Kishore Sahoo, Dr. suresh Nayak, Bharat Majhi, Preetidhara Samal, Ipsita Sarangi, Swapna Mishra, Kishore Panigrahi, Durga Prasad Panda, Manoj Nayak, Saroj Bal, Sitanshu Lenka, Gayatribala Panda, Anirudha Behera etc. This generation is the contemporary poet generation as critics say.

Odia Translation of World Classics

Eminent scholar Prof. Ananta Charan Sukla's celebrated Odia Translation (with Commentary, Critical Study and Notes) of Aristotle's Poetics (Aristotle-anka Kabyatatwa) published in the late 1960s is a rare and outstanding work. It is the second translation of the classic work in any Indian language after Bengali. His translation of four classic Greek plays is also a commendable work.

Fiction

Before the 1970s

In the post-independence era Odia fiction took a new direction. The trend Fakir Mohan started developed more after independence, led by Gopinath Mohanty (1914–1991), Surendra Mohanty and Manoj Das (1934-). These authors pioneered the trend of developing or projecting the "individual as protagonist" in Odia fiction. There is some tension between the two Mohantys among critics. Eminent feminist writer and critic Sarojini Sahoo believes that it is not Gopinath's story "Dan", but rather Surendra Mohanty's "Ruti O Chandra" that should be considered the first story of the individualistic approach. The major difference between Surendra and Gopinath is that, where Gopinath is more optimistic, Surendra is nihilistic. This nihilism prepared the ground for the development an existentialist movement in Odia literature.

Surendra Mohanty is a master of language, theme and concept. Some of his famous short story collections and novels are *Krushna Chuda, Mahanagarira Rati, Ruti O Chandra, Maralara Mrutyu, Shesha Kabita, Dura Simanta, Oh Calcutta, Kabi-O- Nartaki, Sabuja Patra-O-Dhusara Golap, Nila Shaila* and *Andha Diganta*.

In his fiction Gopinath Mohanty explores all aspects of Odishan life, both in the plains and in the hills. He uses a unique prose style, lyrical in style, choosing worlds and phrases from the day-to-day speech of ordinary men and women. Gopinath's first novel, *Mana Gahtra Chasa*, was published in 1940, followed by Dadi Budha (1944), Paraja (1945) and Amrutara Santan (1947). He published 24 novels, 10 collections of short stories, three plays, two biographies, two volumes of critical essays and five books on the languages of Kandh, Gadaba and Saora tribes. He also translated Tolstoy's *War and Peace* (*Yuddh O Shanti*) in three volumes (tr. 1985-86) and Togore's *Jogajog* (tr. 1965) into Odia.

The writer Kalpanakumari Devi's sequence of novels, in particular, her *Srushti o pralaya* (1959), documenting the social change in the country have been lauded.

Starting his literary career as a communist and later becoming an Aurobindian philosopher, Manoj Das proved himself as a successful bilingual writer in Odia and English. His major Odia works are: *Shesha Basantara Chithi* (1966), *Manoj Dasanka Katha O Kahani* (1971), *Dhumabha Diganta* (1971), *Manojpancabimsati* (1977) and *Tuma Gam O Anyanya Kabita*(1992). Notable English works include *The crocodile's lady : a collection of stories* (1975), *The submerged valley and other stories, Farewell to a ghost : short stories and a novelette*(1994), *Cyclones* (1987) and *A tiger at twilight* (1991). Renowned writer Ananta Charan Sukla's short story collection, "Sulataku Sesa Chitthi" (Last Letter to Sulata) published in 1965 is also worth mentioning. The ten stories included in this book are "Sulataku Sesa Chitthi", "Kapilas", "Janeika Kulapati-nka Mrutyu", "Tandril

Ru Tornoto", "Mystic Realistic", "Prasanta Samudra: Asanta Lahari", "Nalakula Matha, Nepala Babu O Narana", "Daudana Bada Khara", "Duragata" and "Sandipani-ra Symphony". Other significant pre-1970s fiction writers are Chandrasekhar Rath, Shantanu Kumar Acharya, Mohapatra Nilamani Sahoo, Akhil Mohan Patnaik, Gobind Das, Rabi Patnaik and JP Das. Chandra Sekhar Rath's novel *Jantrarudha* is one of the renowned classics of this period. Shantanu Acharya's novel Nara-Kinnara was also influential.

After the 1970s

The trends started by the 1950s and 1960s were challenged by the young writers in the 1970s. This challenge began in the 1960s with a small magazine *Uan Neo Lu* in Cuttack. The title of the magazine was made up of three of the Odia alphabets, which were not in use. Writers associated with the magazines included Annada Prasad Ray, Guru Mohanty (not to be confused with Guru Prasad), Kailash Lenka and Akshyay Mohanty. These writers were not as famous as some contemporaries, but they began a revolution in Odia fiction. They tried to break the monopoly of established writers, introducing sexuality in their work and creating a new prose style. In the late 1960s the Cuttack's in Odia Literature was broken when many "groups" of writers emerged from different parts of Odisha. Anamas from Puri, Abadhutas from Balugaon, Panchamukhi from Balangir, Abujha from Berhampur and Akshara group from Sambalpur created a sensation in Odia literary scene.

The changes that started in the 1960s were confirmed in the next decade. Jagadish Mohanty, Kanheilal Das, Satya Mishra, Ramchandra Behera, Tarun Kanti Mishra, Padmaja Pal, Yashodhara Mishra and Sarojini Sahoo created a new era in Odia fiction. Kanheilal Das and Jagadish Mohanty began creating a new style and language popular among a general audience as well as intellectuals. Kanheilal Das died young and is still considered a great loss for Odia fictions. Jagadish Mohanty introduced existentialism to Odia literature. His renowned works include *Ekaki Ashwarohi, Dakshina Duari Ghara, Album, Dipahara Dekhinathiba Lokotie, Nian O Anyanya Galpo, Mephestophelesera Pruthibi, Nija Nija Panipatha, Kanishka Kanishka, Uttaradhikar* and *Adrushya Sakal*.

Ramchandra Behera is known for short story collections *Dwitiya Shmashana, Abashishta Ayusha, Omkara Dhwani, Bhagnangshara Swapna* and *Achinha Pruthibi*. Padmaj Pal is also known for short story collections including *Eaglera Nakha Danta, Sabuthu Sundar Pakshi, Jibanamaya* and *Uttara Purusha*. Tarun Kanti Mishra emerged during 1970s as a powerful storyteller with an elegant style, full of poise and vigor. His outstanding works include 'Sharadah Shatam' (A Thousand Autumns), - a novel dealing with resettlement and rehabilitation of displaced persons from East Pakistan, now Bangladesh - and anthologies of short stories such as 'Komal Gandhar', 'Bitansa', 'Bhaswati' and 'Akash Setu'.

Sarojini Sahoo, another prominent writer, later famous as a feminist writer, also significantly contributed to Odia fiction. Her novel *Gambhiri Ghara* is not only a landmark Odia novel but has also gained international fame for its feminist and liberal ideas. Her other works include *Amrutara Pratikshare, Chowkatha, Upanibesh, Pratibandi, Paksibasa, Tarlijauthiba Durga, Dukha Apramita, Gambhiri Ghara* and *Mahajatra*. Kanaklata Hati, another women fiction writer in whose writing we will find psychoanalysis of female mind. To date she has published two story collections- 'Nirbak Pahada' & 'Kuhudi Ghara'. She has some translated story collections like 'Galpa Galpantara' and'Praibeshi Galpa'.

Popular fiction writings

A popular Odia literature also emerged in the 1970s, read by rural populace especially women. The best selling writers are Bhagirathi Das, Kanduri Das, Bhagwana Das, Bibhuti Patnaik and Pratibha Ray. Some of their works were made into films in the Odia language. In recent times Rabi Kaunungo, Tarun Kanti Mishra, Ajay Swain, Mrinal Chatterjee, Radhu Mishra, Dr Laxmikant Tripathy, Nisith Bose, Suniti Mund, Anjan Chand and Dr. Kulangara have contributed to popular writing.

Women's writings and feminism

The founding of a women's magazine called *Sucharita* in 1975 by Sakuntala Panda had a significant impact in helping female writers find a voice. Some of those writers are Giribala Mohanty, Jayanti Rath, Susmita Bagchi. Paramita Satpathy, Hiranmayee Mishra, Chirashree Indra Singh, Sairindhree Sahoo, Supriya Panda, Gayatri Saraf, Suniti Mund and Mamatamayi Chowdhry.

Giribala Mohanty(1947-) needs a special introduction for her deep sensitiveness for the women issues.Her poems depict the emotional binary of social apathy and the self-confidence of women.Her collections of Poems 'Streeloka'(Women), 'Kalijhia'(The Dark complexion Girl),'Ma Habara Dukha'(The sorrow of being a mother)and 'Kati Katia Katyayani' expresses her feelings in a lucid and lyrical way.Sarojini Sahoo had a significant influence on these women, paving the way with a feminist approach to fiction and the introduction of sexuality in her work.

She is known as the Simone de Beauvoir of India, though theoretically she denies the Hegelian theory of "Other" developed by de Beauvoir in her *The Second Sex*. Unlike de Beauvoir, Sahoo claims that women are an "Other" from the masculine perspective, but that they are entitled to equal human rights according to Plato. Suniti Mund's Story Book 'Anustupa', Poetry Book 'Jhia' And Novel 'Abhisapta', 'Agarbatira Ghara', 'Matrimony dot com','Gigolo' is also feminism voice.

Drama

The traditional Odia theater is the folk opera, or Jatra, which flourishes in the rural areas of Odisha. Modern theater is no longer commercially viable, but in the 1960 experimental theatre made a mark through the works of Manoranjan Das, who pioneered a new theater movement with his brand of experimentalism.

Bijay Mishra, Biswajit Das, Kartik Rath, Ramesh Prasad Panigrahi, Ratnakar Chaini, Prasanna Das, Pramod Kumar Tripathy, Sankar Tripathy, Ranjit Patnaik, Dr. Pradip Bhowmic, Hemendra Mahapatra, and Purna Chandra Mallick continued the tradition.

Tripathy's contribution to the growth and development of the immensely popular and thought-provoking *lok natakas* is universally recognised and he is often called the Rousseau of lok natakas. Noted writer Ananta Charan Sukla's Odia translation of four classic Greek dramas is a rare contribution to Odia drama literature. His book, "Greek Drama", published in 1974, has translations (with commentary) of Prometheus Bound (by Aeschylus), Oedipus the King (by Sophocles), Medea (by Euripides) and The Frogs (by Aristophanes). Sukla's translations of the plays have been staged in various colleges and universities of Odisha. Besides, his two historical plays on Odia freedom fighters Chakhi Khuntia and Jayee Rajguru have also been widely staged. Though there is no commercially viable modern Odia theater, there are amateur theater groups and drama competitions. Operas, on the other hand, are commercially successful.

Popular science fiction writers from Odisha

Some popular science fiction writers include Prof Prana Krushna Parija, Padmashree Binod Kanungo, Prof Gokulananda Mohapatra, Prof Gadadhar Mishra, Prof Kulamani Samal, Sarat Kumar Mohanty, Prof Amulya Kumar Panda, Dr. Nikhilanand Panigrahy, Dr. Debakanta Mishra, Dr.Ramesh Chandra Parida, Sashibhusan Rath, Dr. Chitta Ranjan Mishra, Dr. Nityananada Swain, Dr. Choudhury Satybrata Nanda, Er. Mayadhar Swain, Kamalakanta Jena, Himansu Sekhar Fatesingh and Bibhuprasad Mohapatra etc.

Dr. Nikhilanand Panigrahy's "Sampratikatara Anuchintare

Bigyan O Baigyanik" is a popular book among avid readers. Sashibhusan Rath's *Vigyan Chinta* and Kamalakanta Jena's *Gapare Gapare Bigyan* (Awarded by Odisha Bigyan Academy 2011) are written for children as well as adults.

In the United States

A large initiative, Pratishruti, was started to connect literary minded people in North America with their Indian peers. The goal is to expose Indian-Americans to the best writings of outstanding Odia writers as well as to cultivate new writers in America.

5

Geography and Flora & Fauna

GEOGRAPHY

Mahanadi river near Cuttack

Odisha lies between the latitudes 17.780N and 22.730N, and between longitudes 81.37E and 87.53E. The state has an area of 155,707 km, which is 4.87% of total area of India, and a coastline of 45 km.

In the eastern part of the state lies the coastal plain. It extends from the Subarnarekha River in the north to the Rushikulya river in the south. The lake Chilika is part of the coastal plains.

The plains are rich in fertile silt deposited by the six major rivers flowing into the Bay of Bengal: Subarnarekha, Budhabalanga, Baitarani, Brahmani, Mahanadi and Rushikulya. The Central Rice Research Institute (CRRI), a Food and Agriculture Organization-recognised rice gene bank and research institute, is situated on the banks of Mahanadi in Cuttack.

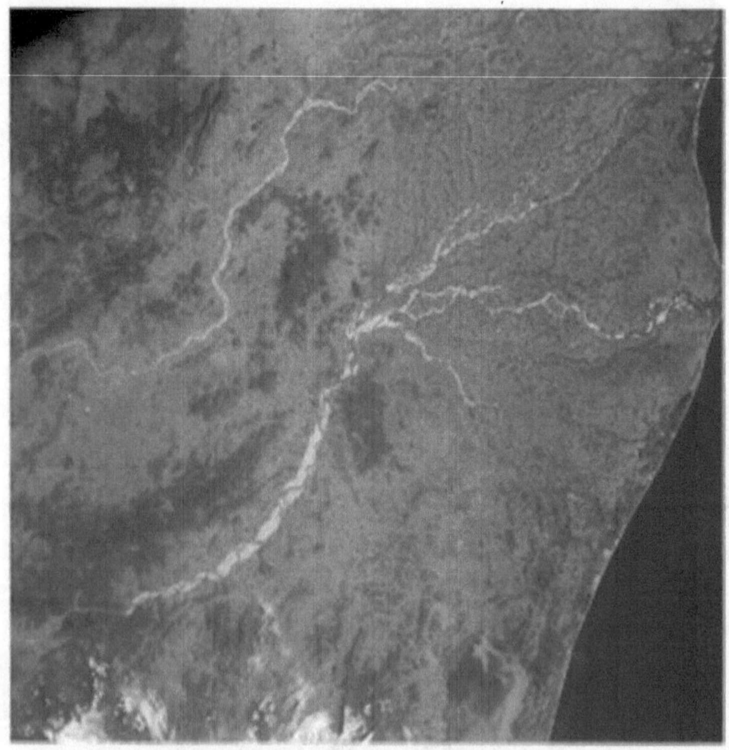

Satellite view of the Mahanadiriver delta

Three-quarters of the state is covered in mountain ranges. Deep and broad valleys have been made in them by rivers. These valleys have fertile soil and are densely populated. Odisha also has plateaus and rolling uplands, which have lower elevation than the plateaus.

The highest point in the state is Deomaliat 1672 metres. The other high peaks are: Sinkaram (1620 m), Golikoda (1617 m), and Yendrika (1582 metres).

Climate

The state experiences four meteorological seasons: winter (January to February), pre-monsoon season (March to May), south-west monsoon season (June to September) and north east monsoon season (October–December). However, locally the year is divided into six traditional seasons (or *rutus*): *Basanta* (spring), *Grishma* (summer), *Barsha* (rainy season), *Sharad* (autumn), *Hemant* (winter), and *Sisira*(cool season).

Biodiversity

Irrawaddy dolphins can be found in Chilika (Note: This is a picture taken from Cambodia.)

Vanda tessellata, *one of the orchids found in Odisha*

Birds at Chilika Lake

Crocodile in Bhitarkanika National Park

White tiger in the Nandankanan Zoo

According to a Forest Survey of India report released in 2012, Odisha has 48,903 km^2 of forests which cover 31.41% of the state's total area. The forests are classified into: dense forest (7,060 km^2), medium dense forest (21,366 km^2), open forest (forest without closed canopy; 20,477 km^2) and scrub forest(4,734 km^2). The state also has bamboo forests (10,518 km^2) and mangroves (221 km^2). The state is losing its forests to timber smuggling, mining, industrialisation and grazing. There have been attempts at conservation and reforestation.

Due to the climate and good rainfall, Odisha's evergreen and moist forests are suitable habitats for wild orchids. Around 130 species have been reported from the state. 97 of them are found in Mayurbhanj district alone. The Orchid House of Nandakanan Biological Park hosts some of these species.

Simlipal National Park is a protected wildlife area and tiger reserve spread over 2750 km of the northern part of Mayurbhanj district. It has 1078 species of plants, including 94 orchids. The sal tree is the primary tree species there. The park has 55 mammals, including barking deer, Bengal tiger, common langur, four-horned antelope, Indian bison, Indian elephant, Indian giant squirrel, Indian leopard, jungle cat, sambar deer, and wild boar. There are 304 species of birds in the park, such as the common hill myna, grey hornbill, Indian pied hornbill and Malabar pied hornbill. It also has 60 species of reptiles, notable among which are the king cobra and tricarinate hill turtle. There is also a mugger crocodile breeding program in nearby Ramtirtha. The Chandaka Elephant Sanctuary is a 190 km protected area near the capital city, Bhubaneswar. However, urban expansion and over-grazing have reduced the forests and are driving herds of elephants to migration. In 2002, there were about 80 elephants. But by 2012, their numbers had been reduced to 20. Many of the animals have migrated toward the Barbara reserve forest, Chilika, Nayagarh district, and Athagad. Some elephants have died in conflicts with villagers, while some have died during migration from being electrocuted by power lines or hit by trains. Outside the protected area, they are killed by poachers. Besides elephants, the sanctuary also has Indian leopards, jungle cats and chitals.

The Bhitarkanika National Park in Kendrapara District covers 650 km, of which 150 km are mangroves. The Gahiramatha beach in Bhitarkanika is the world's largest nesting site for olive ridley sea turtles.Other major nesting grounds for the turtle in the state are Rushikulya, in Ganjam district, and the mouth of the Devi river. The Bhitarkanika sanctuary is also noted for its large population of salt-water crocodiles. In winter, the sanctuary is also visited by migratory birds. Among the species of birds spotted in the sanctuary are the black-crowned night heron, darter, grey heron, Indian cormorant, Oriental white ibis, purple heron, and sarus crane. The possibly endangered horseshoe crab is also found in this region.

Chilika Lake is a brackish water lagoon on the east coast of Odisha with an area of 1105 km. It is connected to the Bay of Bengal by a 35-km-long narrow channel and is a part of the Mahanadi delta. In the dry season, the tides bring in salt water. In the rainy season, the rivers falling into the lagoon decrease its salinity. Birds from places like the Caspian Sea, Lake Baikal, other parts of Russia, Central Asia, South-East Asia, Ladakh and the Himalayas migrate to the lagoon in winter. Among the birds spotted there are Eurasian wigeon, pintail, bar-headed goose, greylag goose, flamingo, mallard and Goliath heron. The lagoon also has a small population of the endangered Irrawaddy dolphins. The state's coastal region has also had sightings of finless porpoise, bottlenose dolphin, humpback dolphin and spinner dolphin in its waters.

FLORA AND FAUNA OF ODISHA

The flora and fauna of Odisha, a state in eastern India, is extremely diverse and gives the state a reputation for abundance of natural beauty and wildlife.

The districts in the interior are thickly covered by forests both of the tropical moist deciduous type as well as tropical dry deciduous. The hills, plateaus and isolated areas of the northeastern part of the state are covered by the tropical moist deciduous forests whereas the second types of the forests are located in the southwest region of the state.

A langur

Some of the trees which grow in abundance in Odisha are bamboo, teak, rosewood, sal, piasal, sanghvan and haldi. There are 479 species of birds, 86 species of mammals, 19 species of amphibians and 110 species of reptiles present in Odisha. The state is also an important habitat for the endangered olive ridley turtles and Irrawaddy dolphins. Koraft district of southern Odisha has been identified by Food and Agriculture Organisation

(FAO) of UN as Global Agricultural Heritage site which is among only other three sites in the world.Other sites are in Peru, China and Philippines.

Flora

Almost one-third of Odisha is covered by forests which make up about 37.34% of the total land area of the state. These forests cover most of southern and western Odisha. The eastern plains adjacent to the coast are covered by farmlands.

The forest cover of Odisha extends over an area of 58,136.869 square kilometres out of which reserve forests make up an area of 26,329.12 square kilometres (10,165.73 sq mi), demarcated protected forests make up 11,687.079 square kilometres (4,512.406 sq mi) and undemarcated protected forests make up 3,638.78 square kilometres (1,404.94 sq mi). Other types of forests make up 16,261.34 square kilometres (6,278.54 sq mi) while unclassed forests make up 20.55 square kilometres (7.93 sq mi) of the total forest cover.

The State Government of Odisha also classifies forests based on their density. About 538 square kilometres (208 sq mi) of land are classified as very dense forests with a canopy density of over 70 percent, 27,656 square kilometres (10,678 sq mi) of forests are classified as moderately dense cover with a canopy density of 40 to 70 percent and 20,180 square kilometres (7,790 sq mi) of land are classified as open forest with a canopy density of 10 to 40 percent.

Odisha has a diverse variety of plants and animals. Odisha's forests yield large quantities of teak and bamboo. Teak, apart from medicinal plants and kendu leaves contribute substantially towards Odisha's economy. Odisha's forest ecosystem has been greatly affected by deforestation and illegal smuggling and poaching.

The state government has established the Odisha Forest Development Corporation to combat the menace of smuggling. The State Pollution Control Board has brought a set of rules to force in order to combat environmental pollution.

Chilka Lake

Sanderlings at Chilka Lake

In 1981, Chilika Lake was designated the first Indian wetland of international importance under the Ramsar Convention due to its rich biodiversity. Over a million migratory waterfowl and shorebirds winter here including many rare and endangered species. The lake is of great value in preserving genetic diversity and over 400 vertebrate species have been recorded.

However conflicts have arisen over the ecosystem of the lake such as Siltation, and disagreements between fisherman, resulting in an overall loss of biodiversity. As a result, the Odisha State Government with support from the Government of India adopt adaptive conservation and management actions. In 1992, the Government of Odisha, concerned by the degradation of the lake's ecosystem, established the Chilika Development Authority (CDA) for the restoration and overall development of the lake under the Indian Societies Registration Act. An Integrated Management Plan was later implemented with financial support of Rs570 million (US $12.7 million) and Hydrobiological monitoring was supported under the Odisha Water Resources Consolidation Project of the World Bank, to the extent of Rs10 million (US $220,000). A strong support network was created with 7 state government organisations, 33 NGOs, 3 National Government Ministries, 6 other organisations, 11 International organisations, 13 research institutions and 55 different categories of community groups established good international contacts for protection in the area.

Chilika Sea mouth

In November 2002, the Ramsar Wetland Conservation Award was presented to the Chilika Development Authority for "outstanding achievements in the field of restoration and wise use of wetlands and effective participation of local communities in these activities".

The ecological richness of the lake is of great value in preserving the genetic diversity because of the multiplicity of its habitat, flora and fauna. (Some are pictured in the photo gallery). The Zoological Survey of India (ZSI) surveyed the lake between 1985 and 1988 and identified 800 species of fauna, including many rare, endangered, threatened and vulnerable species, but excluding terrestrial insects.

The rare and threatened animal species identified are green sea turtle (EN), dugong (VU), Irrawaddy dolphin (VU), blackbuck (NT), spoon billed sandpiper (CR), limbless skink and fishing cat (EN). 24 mammalian species were reported. 37 species of reptiles and amphibians are also reported.

Flora

Recent surveys revealed an overall 726 species of flowering plants belonging to 496 genera and 120 families. This represents about one–fourth of the vascular plant species of the Odisha state where some 2900 species altogether are found. Fabaceae is the most dominant plant family followed by Poaceae and Cyperaceae. Certain species were found to be characteristic of specific islands. Important species identified are:.

- Leguminosae, Poaceae, and Cyperaceae
- Endemic cassipourea ceylanica
- Five species of seagrass
- Wild plants of horticultural importance and interesting plant groups such as insectivorous plants, epiphytes, parasites and lithophytes
- Mangrove associates, such as Aegiceras corniculatus, Excoecaria agalloch, Salvadora persica, Pongamia pinnata, Colubrina asiatica, Capparis roxburghii, Macrotyloma ciliatum and many others.

Aviffauna

Chilika Lake is the largest wintering ground for migratory birds, on the Indian sub-continent. It is one of the hotspots of biodiversity in the country. Some species listed in the IUCN Red List of Threatened Species inhabit the lake for at least part of their lifecycle.

Migratory water fowl arrive here from as far as the Caspian Sea, Baikal Lake and remote parts of Russia, Mongolia, Lakah, Siberia, Iran, Iraq, Afghanistan and from the Himalayas.A census conducted in the winter of 1997–98 recorded about 2 million birds in the lake.

In 2007, nearly 840,000 birds visited the lake, out of which 198,000 were spotted in Nalbana Island. On 5 January 2008, a bird census involving 85 wildlife officials counted 900,000 birds of which 450,000 were sighted in Nalabana. Removal of invasive species of freshwater aquatic plants, especially water hyacinth, due to restoration of salinity, is a contributing factor for the recent increasing attraction of birds to the lake.

Goliath heron

Nalbana Island is the core area of the Ramsar designated wetlands of Chilika Lake. Nalbana means *a weed covered island* In the Odia language. It is a major island in the centre of the lake and has an area of 15.53 km (6.0 sq mi). The island gets completely submerged during the monsoon season. As the monsoon recedes in the winter, lake levels decrease and the island is gradually exposed, birds flock to the island in large numbers to feed on its extensive mudflats. Nalbana was notified in 1987 and declared a bird sanctuary in 1973 under the Wildlife Protection Act.

Large flocks of greater flamingos from Iran and the Rann of Kutch in Gujarat, feed in the shallow waters of the lake. Other long legged waders seen around Nalbana Island are the lesser flamingos, Goliath herons, grey herons, and purple herons, egrets, spoonbills, storks and black-headed ibis.

Rare birds reported in the lake are Asiatic dowitchers (NT), Dalmatian pelican (VU), Pallas's fish-eagles (VU), the very rare migrant spoon-billed sandpiper (CR) and spot-billed pelican (NT).

The white-bellied sea eagle, pariah kite, brahminy kites, kestrel, marsh harriers, and the world's most widespread bird of prey, the peregrine falcon, are among the raptors seen here.

Many short-legged shorebirds are seen in a narrow band along the shifting shores of the lake and islands. These include plovers, the collared pratincole, ruff, dunlin, snipes and sandpipers. larks, wagtails and lapwings are also found on the mudflats. Feeding in deeper water are the longer-legged avocets, stilts and godwits.

The higher vegetated areas of the lake support moorhens, coots and jacanas. Pond herons and night herons can be seen along the shores with kingfishers and rollers. Little cormorants are seen on perches around the lake. Compact flocks of brahminy ducks, as well as shovellers, pintails, gadwall, teals, pochards, geese and coots, are also seen.

Nesting colonies of gull-billed terns and river terns are seen on the Nalabana Island. In 2002, the Bombay Natural History Society survey recorded 540 nests of the Indian river tern at the island, the largest nesting colony in the southeast Asia.

Aquafauna

As per the Chilika Development Authority's (CDA) updated data (2002), 323 aquatic species, which includes 261 fish species, 28 prawns and 34 crabs are reported out of which sixty five species breed in the lake. 27 species are freshwater fishes and two genera of prawns. The remaining species migrate to the sea to breed. 21 species of herrings and sardines of the family Clupeidae are reported.

Between 1998–2002, 40 fish species were recorded here for

the first time and following the reopening of the lake mouth in 2000, six threatened species have reappeared, including:

- Milk fish (Seba khainga),
- Indo-Pacific tarpon (Panialehio),
- Ten pounder (Nahama),
- Bream (Kala khuranti),
- Hilsa (Tenuealosa) ilisha (ilishi) and
- Mullet *R. corsula* (Kekenda)

Commercial fisheries

For centuries fisher folk evolved exclusive rights of fishing through a complex system of partitioning the fisheries of the lake, harvested the lake in a relatively sustainable fashion and developed a large range of fishing techniques, nets and gear.

During the British rule, in 1897–98, fishermen community enjoyed exclusive fisheries rights in the lake. The fisheries of the lake were part of the Zamindari estates of Khallikote, Parikud, Suna Bibi, Mirza Taher Baig and the Chaudhary families of Bhungarpur and the Khas mahal areas of Khurda, lying within the kingdoms of the Rajas of Parikud and Khallikote. The zamindars (Landlords) leased out the fisheries exclusively to the local fisherfolk.

With the abolition of zamindari (land lordship) system in 1953, traditional fishing areas continued to be leased out to cooperatives of local fishermen. Fishing, particularly, prawn fishing, became increasingly remunerative with outside interest playing an important role. But in 1991, when the government of Odisha proposed a leasing policy that would have resulted in the auction of leases to the highest bidder, fishermen's cooperatives challenged the order in court. The High Court of Odisha ordered the Government to enact changes that would protect the interests of traditional fishermen and since then no new leases have been reported. This has resulted in a chaotic regime in which powerful vested interests from outside dominate, and the local people have been subordinated.

Butter catfish and *Wallago attu* are the most common type of fish found in the lake. 11 species of fish, 5 species of prawn and 2 crab species are commercially important. The commercially important prawn are giant tiger prawn, *Penaeus indicus* (Indian white shrimp), *Metapenaeus monoceros* (speckled shrimp), *Metapenaeus affinis* (pink prawn) and *Metapenaeus dobson* (Kadal shrimp). Mangrove crab is the most important commercial crab. Fish landings in the lake, which fluctuated in the past, have recorded a remarkable recovery after the opening of the new mouth and dredging of silt –choked old mouth Magarmukh in 2000–2001, resulted in a better intermixing of the tidal influx from the sea and freshwater inflow from rivers. Against an all time lowest landing of fish and prawn of 1269 MT 1,269 t (1,398.8 short tons) in 1995–96, the all-time high is reported to be 11,878 t (13,093.3 short tons) during 2001–2002 resulting in an estimated per capita income for the fisher folk of Rs19,575 (about US $392) during the year. Recently, the Government of Odisha have issued a notification banning the lease of Chilika Lake for Culture Fishery.

Dolphins

The Irrawaddy dolphin (*Orcaella brevirostris*) is the flagship species of Chilika lake. Chilka is home to the only known population of Irrawaddy dolphins in India and one of only two lagoons in the world that are home to this species. It is classified as Critically Endangered, in five of the six other places it is known to live.

A small population of bottlenose dolphins, also migrate into the lagoon from the sea. Chilika fishermen say that when Irrawaddy dolphins and bottlenose dolphins meet in the outer channel, the former get frightened and are forced to return toward the lake.

Some Irrawaddy dolphins used to be sighted only along the inlet channel and in a limited portion of the central sector of the lake. After the opening of the new mouth at Satapada in 2000, they are now well distributed in the central and the southern sector of the lake. The number of dolphins sighted has varied from 50 to 170. A 2006 census counted 131 dolphins and the 2007 census revealed 138 dolphins. Out of the 138 dolphins, 115 were adults, 17 adolescents and six calves. 60 adults were spotted in the outer channel followed by 32 in the central sector and 23 in the southern sector.

Dolphin tourism provides an important alternative source of income for many local residents. There are four tourist associations in Satapada employing three hundred and sixty 9-HP long-tail motor boats taking tourists to a 25 km (9.7 sq mi) area of the lake for dolphin watching. About 500 fishing families are involved in this business. The Odisha Tourism Department and the Dolphin Motorboat Association, an NGO at Satpada, report about 40,000 tourists visit Chilika every year for dolphin Watching. October–January and May–June are the peak season for tourists at Chilika, with a maximum 600–700 per day during December–January. The Dolphin Motorboat Association has 75 8-passenger motorboats for dolphin watching. Tourists pay Rs.250 for 60–90 minutes per trip. According to the Association, most tourists see dolphins. Only 5% return disappointed. Besides the Association, the Odisha Tourism Department organises "dolphin-watch" for tourists. Even during monsoon, about 100 tourists/day visit the lake.

Boat based dolphin watching tours impact dolphin behavior and cause several accidental dolphin deaths each year. CDA conducts an annual census of dolphin deaths. They report 15 deaths in 2003–04, 11 in 2004–05, 8 in 2005–06 and 5 in 2006–07. 40% of the 2006–07 deaths were by mechanised boats.

Since 1984, the Whale and Dolphin Conservation Society has been conducting a science-based community education project to conserve the Irrawaddy dolphins and Chilika Lake. They have determined the primary cause of mortality for this population of dolphins is floating gill nets and hook line fisheries and the secondary cause is boat strikes from increasing unmanaged tourism activities. The Irrawaddy dolphins have a seemingly mutualistic relationship of co-operative fishing with the traditional fishermen. Fishermen recall when they would call out to the dolphins, to drive fish into their nets. Castnet fishing with the help of Irrawaddy dolphins in upper reaches of the Ayeyawady River has been well documented.

The only other sub-populations of Irrawaddy dolphins are found in a 190 km (118.1 mi) stretch of the Mekong River in Lao PDR and Cambodia (about 70–100 freshwater individuals); in a 420 km (261.0 mi) stretch of the Mahakam River, Indonesia (about 33–50 freshwater individuals); Malampaya Sound, Philippines (about 77 individuals) and in a 370 km (229.9 mi) stretch of the Ayeyarwady River in Myanmar (about 59 freshwater individuals). Less than 50 were reported in Songkhla Lake in Thailand. With no more than 474 Irrawaddy dolphins reported worldwide in 2007, The Chilika dolphins comprise at least 29% of the total world population and are the largest subpopulation in the world.

FORESTS IN ODISHA

Tropical-moist-deciduous forests in Odisha

Dry evergreen forests during monsoon

Forests

There are two basic kinds of forest here; in the northeast region of the state the forest is classified as the tropical-moist-deciduous type, blanketing hills, plateaus and other high-altitude isolated areas; in the southwest the tropical-dry-deciduous variety dominate. Orissa's forests are vast. Out of the total geographical area of 155,707 km, the State records 52,472 km (~33%) as some version of forest. The actual forest cover may be less, according to the Forest Survey of India, rosewood, sal, piasal, sanghvan and haldi. The forest's naturally vigorous growth accounts for a tremendous wealth of biodiversity, filling many catalogues of the wild plant and animal species dwelling within.

The state has declared large parcels of land as protected areas with the purpose being to allow animals and plants who are sensitive to cohabitation with humans places of relative freedom from interference and habitat loss. These protected areas constitute 10.37% of the total forest area and 4.1% of the total geographical area of the state.

Forest flora

The state is home of ca 3000 plant species including 120 orchid species and 63 varieties of mangrove trees which make the state second largest mangrove ecosystem in India.

A vast variety of other plants are also found in the state, as in the following:

* *Acorous calamus*
* *Aegiceras corniculatus*
* *Alpinia galanga* - greater galingal
* *Androgaphis paniculata*
* *Asparagus racemosus* - shatavari
* *Cathraranthus roseus*
* *Celastrus paniculatus*
* *Centella asiatica*
* *Cissus quadranggularis*
* *Clerodendrum* ssp.
* *Colchicum autumnale* - autumn crocus
* *Commiphora wightii* - Mukul myrrh
* *Croton roxburghjii*
* *Curcuma angustifolia*
* *Digitalis purpurea* - common foxglove
* Diogenin
* Emetin
* *Ephedra* ssp.
* *Erythroxylon coca* - coca
* *Excoecaria agallochi*
* *Gloriosa superba*
* Gugulipid
* *Hemidesmus indicus*
* *Ocimum basilicum*
* *Plumbago zeylanica*
* *Pongamia pinnata*

- *Rauwolfia serpentina* - Indian snakeroot
- *Salvadora persica*
- seagrass
- *Taxus brevifolia* - Pacific yew
- *Toddalia asiatica*
- *Vinblastim areteminsinine*
- *Whighina somenifera*

Forest fauna

The IUCN Red List has recorded a total of 473 species of birds and 86 species of mammals, 19 species of amphibians and 110 species of reptiles including three crocodilian species. Out of these around 54 species are considered endangered. Home to a variety of wild animals, the state has declared considerable tracts of land as areas protected for these animals only. These protected areas constitute 10.37% of the total forest area and 4.1% of the total geographical area of the state. Not only this, the state also has the distinction of possessing three mass nesting beaches of endangered olive ridley sea turtles which makes it the largest nesting ground of the species.

The state has three mass nesting beaches of endangered olive ridley sea turtles which when combined together makes it the world's largest nesting ground for this species.

Indenting Orissa's ocean coast is Chilika lagoon, a semi-saline wetland used by many species of migratory birds, and also which the endangered Irrawaddy dolphin uses as part of its range. In spite of considerable human interactivity here, the rare dolphin survives. The Orissa government is conducting various programs to protect the species.

6

Economy

INTRODUCTION

Macro-economic trend

Odisha is experiencing steady economic growth. The impressive growth in gross domestic product of the state has been reported by the Ministry of Statistics and Programme Implementation. Odisha's growth rate is above the national average. The central Government's Urban Development Ministry has recently announced the names of 20 cities selected to be developed as smart cities. The state capital Bhubaneswar is the first city in the list of smart Cities released in January 2016, a pet project of Prime Minister Narendra Modi. The announcement also marked with sanction of Rs 50,802 crore over the five years for development.

Industrial development

Odisha has abundant natural resources and a large coastline. Odisha has emerged as the most preferred destination for overseas investors with investment proposals. It contains a fifth of India's coal, a quarter of its iron ore, a third of its bauxite reserves and most of the chromite. Rourkela Steel Plant was the first integrated steel plant in the public sector in India, built with collaboration of Germany.

Rourkela Steel Plant

Arcelor-Mittal has also announced plans to invest in another mega steel project amounting to $10 billion. Russian major Magnitogorsk Iron and Steel Company (MMK) plans to set up a 10 MT steel plant in Odisha, too. Bandhabahal is a major area of open cast coal mines in Odisha. The state is attracting an unprecedented amount of investment in aluminium, coal-based power plants, petrochemicals, and information technology as well. In power generation, Reliance Power (Anil Ambani Group) is putting up the world's largest power plant with an investment of US $13 billion at Hirma in Jharsuguda district.

In the year 2009 Odisha was the second top domestic investment destination with Gujarat first and Andhra Pradesh in third place according to an analysis of ASSOCHAM Investment Meter (AIM) study on corporate investments. Odisha's share was 12.6 percent in total investment in the country. It received investment proposal worth . 2,00,846 crore during the last year. Steel and power were among the sectors which attracted maximum investments in the state. Flood and cyclone are the major hurdles in Odisha's development as the important districts are situated near to the Bay of Bengal. In the five-year period between 2004 and 2005 and 2008–09, Odisha's GDP has grown by a stunning 8.74% way beyond the definition of 7% growth. All-India growth during this period was 8.49%. In this period, Odisha was the fourth fastest growing state, just behind Gujarat, Bihar, Uttarakhand.

Transportation

Odisha has a network of roads, railways, airports and seaports. Bhubaneswar is well connected by air, rail and road with the rest of India. Some highways are getting expanded to four lanes. Plans for metro rail connecting Bhubaneshwar and Cuttack, a journey of 30 km, have also started.

Air

Odisha has a total of 17 airstrips and 16 helipads. The Government of Odisha have announced to develop an airport at Jharsuguda, making it a full-fledged domestic airport. Five greenfield airports were also to be upgraded at Angul, Dhamra, Kalinganagar, Paradip and Rayagada in an effort to boost intra-State and inter-State civil aviation. Existing aerodromes at Barbil, Gopalpur, Jharsuguda and Rourkela were also to be upgraded. Air Odisha, is Odisha's sole air charter company based in Bhubaneswar.

- Angul - Savitri Jindal Airport
- Bhawanipatna - Utkela Airstrip
- Bhubaneswar - Biju Patnaik International Airport
- Brahmapur - Berhampur Airport
- Cuttack - Charbatia Air Base
- Jeypore - Jeypore Airport
- Jharsuguda - Jharsuguda Airport
- Rourkela - Rourkela Airport
- Sambalpur - Hirakud Airstrip

Seaports

Gopalpur Port

There are many sea ports in the long seacoast of Odisha. some of them are:

- Port of Dhamara
- Port of Gopalpur
- Port of Paradip
- Port of Subarnarekha

- Port of Astarang
- Port of Chandipur

Railways

East Coast Railway headquarters, Bhubaneswar

Major cities of Odisha are well connected to all the major cities of India by direct daily trains and weekly trains. Most of the railway network in Odisha lies under the jurisdiction of the East Coast Railway (ECoR) with headquarters at Bhubaneswar and some parts under South Eastern Railway and South East Central Railway.

ECONOMY OF ODISHA

The economy of Odisha is one of the fastest growing state economies in India . According to 2014-15 economic survey, Odisha's gross state domestic product (GSDP) was expected to grow at 8.78%. Odisha has an agriculture-based economy which is in transition towards an industry and service-based economy. According to recent estimates, the size of Odisha's economy has increased by 22.27 per cent during the last six years in terms of the gross state domestic product (GSDP). Thereby, Odisha achieved an annual average growth rate of 6.23 per cent during that period. Odisha is also one of the top FDI destinations in India. In the fiscal year 2011-12, Odisha received investment proposals worth 49,527 crore (US$9.296 billion). According to the Reserve Bank of India, It received 53,000 crore (US$8.33 billion) worth of new FDI commitments in the 2012-13 fiscal year.

Overview

In 2013-14, the GSDP growth rate dropped to 2.21%. This slown down was attributed to the Phailin cyclone, which caused a negative growth of 9.78% in the agricultural sector and also affected several other sectors. According to the 2011 Census of India, Odisha has a working population of 17,541,589, among them 61% are main workers and rest are marginal workers. 33.9% of the total working female population are main workers. As of June 2014, Odisha has 10,95,151 people registered in various employment exchanges of the state. Of them, 10,42,826 reported themselves educated. Odisha had a rural unemployment rate of 8.7% and an urban unemployment rate 5.8% calculated based on the current daily status basis in the 68th National Sample Survey (2011-2012). The per capita income of the state was 98,983 (US$1,531) in 2013-14. The state has a public debt of 38,666 crore (US$6.34 billion), which is 8,909 per capita (US$146), at the end of 2013-14.

According to ASSOCHAM, in the fiscal year 2011-12, Odisha received investment proposals worth 49,527 crore (US$9.296 billion). According to the Reserve Bank of India, Odisha received new FDI proposals worth Rs 53,000 crore (8.333 billion USD) in the 2012-13 fiscal year. In 2012-13, 125 crore (US$19.66 million) worth of foreign aid was received by NGOs in the state.

Contribution of each sector to the GSDP (in percent)

Service (51%)

Agriculture (15.4%)

Industry (33.6%)

GSDP by year

Year	GSDP (in crore Indian rupees)
2001-02	46,756
2002-03	49,719
2003-04	61,008
2004-05	77,729
2005-06	85,096

2006-07	101,839
2007-08	129,274
2008-09	148,491
2009-10	162,946
2010-11	197,530
2011-12	214,583
2012-13	255,459
2013-14	288,414
2014-15	310,810
2015-16	348,107

ECONOMIC SECTORS

Agriculture and Livestock

According to the 2011 Census of India, 61.8% of the working population are engaged in agricultural activities. However, the agricultural's contribution to the GSDP was 16.3% in the fiscal year 2013-14 and it was estimated to be 15.4% in 2014-15. The area under cultivation was 5,691 hectares in 2005-06 and it dropped to 5,424 hectares in 2013-14. Rice is the dominant crop in Odisha. It is grown on 77% of the area under cultivation. Odisha produced 8,360 metric tonnes of rice in 2013-14, a drop from 10,210 metric tonnes due the cyclone Phailin. Given below is a table of 2015 national output share of select agricultural crops and allied segments in Odisha based on 2011 prices

Segment	National Share %
Cow pea	45.0
Pumpkin	33.6
Niger seed	30.5
Sweet potato	30.4
San hemp	24.7
Brinjal	14.3
Water melon	12.1
Lemon	11.7

Bitter gourd	11.1
Betel	9.9
Cabbage	8.5
Ber	8.4
Fuel wood	8.4
Linseed	7.8
Cashew nut	7.3
Parmal	7.2
Jackfruit	6.9
Okra	6.8
Sunflower	6.3
Bottle gourd	6.0
Tomato	5.9
Moong	5.8
Paddy	5.6
Arhar	5.5
Mango	5.0

During 2013-14, the state exported 4.13 lakh tonnes and 1,800 crore worth of seafood. In 2014-15, the value of exports rose by 26% to 2,300 crore with 4.67 tonnes being exported. Odisha is the fourth largest shrimp producing state in India. On 22 November 2017, Odisha government decided to launch "Nabakrushna Choudhury Seccha Unnayan Yojana" to provide irrigation facility to about 55,000 hectare of agricultural land across Odisha. The scheme would be implemented with an outlay of Rs 635 crore over a period of three years. Under the scheme, 46,296 hectare command area of 14 major and medium irrigations and 284 minor irrigation projects will be revived.

Industry

The primary industries in Odisha are manufacturing; mining and quarrying; electricity, gas and water supply and construction. The industrial sector's contribution to the state's GSDP was estimated at 33.45% in 2014-15. Most of Odisha's industries are mineral-based. Odisha has 25% of India's iron reserves. It has 10% of India's production capacity in steel. Odisha is the top aluminium producing state in India. Two of the largest aluminium plants in India are in Odisha, NALCO and Vedanta Resources. Mining contributed an estimated 6.31% to the GSDP.

Power

Odisha has 9036.36 MW installed capacity of electricity production, out of which 6753.04 MW is coal-generated. 2166.93 MW is generated by hydro power and 116.39 MW by other renewable sources.

Odisha was the first state in India to reform its power sector. In 1996, it passed the Orissa Electricity Reform Act to restructure and privatize the sector. Before the Act, the single public-sector company Orissa State Electricity Board (OSEB) had been producing and supplying electricity in the state since its establishment in 1961. But by 1994-95, OSEB had run into heavy losses and there was a gap of 45% between consumption and production. The reforms unbundled power generation from transmission and distribution. Following the reforms, hydro power plants were handed over to Odisha Hydro Power Corporation (OHPC) and the existing thermal power plants were transferred to Odisha Power Generation Corporation (OPGC). Grid Corporation of Odisha (Gridco) was given the task of power supply. Initially, these were operated as state-owned farms, but later were corporatised.

In August 2014, the government announced a plan to invest 54,000 crore in the power sector over the next 5 years, to provide 24-hours electricity to both the urban and rural regions. Odisha expects to reach a power surplus during its peak consumption months by 2015-16.

Service

The service sector contributed an estimated 51% to the GSDP in 2014-15. The primary sub-sectors are: community, social and personal services, which contributed 13.45% to the GSDP; trade, hotels and restaurants, which contributed 13.09%;

financial and insurance services, which contributed 13.64%; and transport, storage and communication, which contributed 10.99%. The state has a well-developed banking network compared to many states of India. There is one bank branch for every 12,000 people. 90% of the branches are in the rural region.

Poverty

Despite continuing rapid industrialization and absorption of urban educated populaces into the service sector, poverty remains high in the state. The Reserve Bank of India, in a 2013 report said 32.59 % of the population of the state live below the poverty line. Odisha came in 23rd among states and union territories, on this count.

7

Tourism

TOURISM IN ODISHA

Tourism in Odisha is one of the main contributors to the Economy of Odisha, India, with a 500 km (310 mi) long coastline, towering mountains, serene lakes and frolicking rivers. Odisha is one of the major tourism sectors of India, with various tourists' attractions, ranging from wildlife reserves, beaches, temples, monuments, the arts and festivals. Other than wildlife reserves, beaches, temples, monuments, the arts and festivals, the Odisha Tourism Development Corporation, a Public Sector Undertaking of Government of Odisha, is also developing tourism sector of Odisha and India.

Major attractions

Temples

- Aisanyesvara Siva Temple
- Ajaikapada Bhairava Temple
- Akhadachandi Temple
- Alarnatha Mandira
- Anantasaayi Vishnu Temple
- Ananta Vasudeva Temple
- Annakoteshvara Temple

- Astasambhu Temples
- Baladevjew Temple
- Beleswar Temple
- Bhadrakali Temple, Aharapada
- Bhagabati Temple, Banapur
- Bhandara Ghara Shrine
- Bharati Matha
- Bhattarika Temple
- Bhima Kunda
- Bhringesvara Siva Temple
- Bhrukutesvar Siva Temple
- Bhuvaneshwar Temple, Boudh
- Bhusandeswar Temple, Balasore
- Biraja Temple
- Biranchinarayan Temple, Buguda
- Biranchinarayan Temple, Palia
- Brahma Temple, Bindusagar
- Brahma Temple, Niali
- Brahmeswara Temple
- Budha Ganesha Temple
- Byamokesvara Temple
- Chakra Narasimha Temple
- Chakreshvari Siva Temple
- Champakesvara Siva Temple
- Chandaneswar Temple, Balasore
- Chandrasekhara Mahadeva Temple
- Charchika Temple
- Chateshwar Temple
- Chausathi Jogini Temple
- Chintamanisvara Siva Temple
- Cuttack Chandi Temple
- Devasabha Temple

- Digambara Jaina Temple, Khandagiri
- Dishisvara Siva Temple
- Durga Temple, Baideshwar
- Durga Temple, Motia
- Emar Matha
- Gandhi Garabadu Precinct Vishnu Temple
- Gangesvara Siva Temple
- Godhaneswar temple
- Gosagaresvar Siva Temple
- Govardhana matha
- Gundicha Temple
- Hanuman Temple, Kedara-Gouri
- Harachandi Temple
- Harihara Deula
- Harishankar Temple
- Indralath Temple
- Jaleswar Siva Temple Precinct
- Jagannath Temple, Baripada
- Jagannath Temple, Dharakote
- Jagannath Temple, Koraput
- Jagannath Temple, Nayagarh
- Jagannath Temple, Puri
- Joranda Gadi
- Kakatpur Mangala Temple
- Kalika Siva Temple
- Kanaka Durga, Raulapalli
- Kapilash Temple
- Kapilesvara Siva Temple
- Kedareswar Temple
- Khirachora Gopinatha Temple
- Kichakeshwari Temple
- Konark Sun Temple

- Koneswaram temple
- Kosaleswara temple
- Kotitirtha Tank
- Kukutesvara Tank
- Labesvara Siva Temple
- Ladoo Baba Temple
- Lakhesvara Siva Temple
- Lakhmi Varaha Temple
- Lankeswari Temple
- Lingaraja Temple
- Lokanatha Temple
- Maa Barunei Temple
- Maa Borei Temple
- Maa Brajmakali Temple
- Maa Markama Temple
- Maa Tarini Temple, Ghatgaon
- Madhava Temple
- Madneswar Siva Temple
- Majhighariani Temple
- Mahavinayak Temple
- Mahishamardini Temple
- Mangala Temple
- Mangalesvara Siva Temple
- Manibhadresvara Temple – II
- Manikarnika Tank
- Manikeshwari Temple
- Marichi temple
- Markandeshwar Temple
- Mausimaa Temple
- Mausi Maa Temple
- Metakani Temple
- Mukteswar Temple

- Murga Mahadeva Shrine
- Nagesvara Temple, Bhubaneswar
- Narasimha Temple, Puri
- Nilakantheswar Temple
- Nilamadhav Temple
- Nrusinghanath Temple
- Pabaneswara Temple
- Panchalingeshwar
- Papanasini Siva Temple
- Parsurameswar Temple
- Parsvanath Jain Temple-I
- Parsvanath Jain Temple-II
- Parvati Temple, Odisha
- Patali Srikhetra
- Purvesvara Siva Temple
- Rajarani Temple
- Ramachandi Temple
- Ram Mandir, Janpath
- Rameshwar Deula
- Sakshigopal Temple
- Saptamatruka Temple
- Sarvatresvara Siva Temple
- Sasisena Temple
- Sekhareswar Temple
- Siddhesvara Siva Temple
- Simhachalam Temple
- Simhanath Temple
- Sivatirtha Matha
- Subarnameru Temple
- Subarnesvara Siva Temple
- Suka Temple
- Sukutesvara Temple

- Sundaresvara Tank
- Sureswari temple
- Svapnesvara Siva Temple
- Talesvara Siva Temple
- Taratarini Temple
- Tirthesvara Siva Temple
- Upper Bagh Devi Temple
- Uttaresvara Siva Temple
- Vaital Deula
- Varahanatha Temple
- Varahi Deula, Chaurasi
- Vimala Temple
- Vishnu Temple, Bhubaneswar
- Yameshwar Temple

Beaches

Odisha has a long coastline of 500 km and consists of some of the most beautiful beaches of the world. Exotic beaches of Odisha are the venue of India Surf Festival 2014.

- Chandipur Beach
- Chilika
- Gahirmatha Beach
- Gopalpur Beach
- Konark Beach
- Puri Beach
- Talasari Beach

Monuments

Buddhist monuments

- Dhauli
- Lalitgiri
- Pushpagiri
- Ratnagiri

Jain monuments

- Udayagiri and Khandagiri Caves

Forts

- Barabati Fort
- Chudanga Gada
- Raibania Fort
- Sisupalgarh

Museums

- Odisha State Museum
- Regional Museum of Natural History, Bhubaneswar
- Tribal Research Institute Museum

Flora and fauna

Lakes

Chilika Lake

- Chilka Lake: at the mouth of the Daya River, is Asia's largest brackish water lake and second largest brackish water lake in the world. A bird sanctuary for millions of migratory birds, and is also noted for its population of Irrawaddy dolphins (*Orcaella brevirostris*), the only known population of Irrawaddy dolphins in India. It is one of only two lagoons in the world that are home to these species.

- Kanjia Lake: Lake inside the Nandankanan Zoological Park known for boat riding and scenic beauty situated at Bhubaneswar, Odisha, India.

- Anshupa Lake: a horseshoe shaped fresh water lake on the left bank of the Mahanadi River, opposite Banki in Cuttack district, Odisha, India. Anshupa Lake in Banki is 40 km from the city of Cuttack, which also acts as a shelter for the migratory birds in the wintry weather season.

Waterfalls

- Badaghagara Waterfall
- Barehipani Falls
- Devkund Waterfall
- Duduma Waterfalls
- Joranda Falls
- Khandadhar Falls, Kendujhar
- Khandadhar Falls, Sundagarh
- Koilighugar Waterfall
- Sanaghagara Waterfall
- Dian Jhar (Diudhar waterfall), Cuttack
- Atri
- Deulajhari
- Taptapani
- Tarabalo

Wildlife

White tiger in Nandankanan Zoological Park

Odisha is a remarkable place as it is the home to the royal Bengal tiger, consisting of many sanctuaries and natural scenic spots.

Sanctuaries

- Baisipalli Wildlife Sanctuary
- Balimela Wildlife Sanctuary
- Balukhand-Konark Wildlife Sanctuary
- Bhitarkanika Mangroves
- Bhitarkanika National Park
- Chandaka Elephant Sanctuary
- Debrigarh Wildlife Sanctuary
- Hadgarh Wildlife Sanctuary
- Karlapat Wildlife Sanctuary
- Kondakameru Wildlife Sanctuary
- Lakhari Valley Wildlife Sanctuary

- Nandankanan Zoological Park
- Satkosia Tiger Reserve
- Sunabeda Tiger Reserve

Scenic spots

- Daringbadi
- Barunei
- Dhamra
- Chandbali
- Gupteswar Cave
- Tensa
- Saptasajya
- Satabhaya

Islands

Eco-tourism provides a degree of alternate employment to the local community and generates environmental awareness, among local residents as well as visitors, about the conservation and sensible use of the lake's natural resources. Notable locations within the lake are:

- Ramba Bay at the southern end of the lake with the group of islands including:
- The Becon Island, with an architectural conical pillar (to put a light on the top) built by Mr. Snodgrass, the then collector of Ganjam of the East India Company, on a mass of rock in the Rambha Bay near Ghantasila hill. It is surrounded by the Eastern Ghat.
- The Breakfast Island, pear shaped, known as "Sankuda island", with remnants of a dilapidated bungalow constructed by the King of Kalikote, has rare plants and is full of greenery with appealing flora.
- Honeymoon Island, 5 km (3.1 mi) from Rambha Jetty, known as Barkuda Island, with clear waters has abundant red and green macro algae in the bed is also known for the limbless lizard, an endemic species found here.

Satpada

- Somolo and Dumkudi islands, located in the Central and Southern sectors of the lake, in the backdrop of scenic Khalikotehill range, are inundated remnants of the Eastern Ghats with rich flora and fauna and also known for sighting of Irrawaddy dolphins.

- Birds' island, located in the southern sector of the lake has huge exposed hanging rocks, are painted white due to folic acidof the droppings of the birds and is known for rich algal communities and few mangrove species and also migratory birds in winter.

- Parikud is a group of composite islands in the Garh Krishnaprasad Block for nature lovers and provides an avian spectacle during winter season

- Kalijai Temple located on an island is considered to be the abode of the Goddess Kalijai

- Satpada, at the new mouth of the lake, provides a beautiful view of the lake and also views of the dolphins. Hundreds of boats here provide tours of the lake for tourists.

- Barunkuda, a small island situated near Magarmukh, mouth of the lake, has a temple of Lord Varuna.
- Nabagraha is an ancient deity located along the outer channel.
- Chourbar Shiva Temple is located near Alupatna village, along the outer channel.
- Manikpatna, located on the outer channel has historical evidence of a port which was used for trade with Far East and also has the Bhabakundeswar temple of Lord Shiva, an old Mosque whose entrance door is made of the jaws of the whale.
- Sand-Bar and Mouth of the Lake is a striking and un-explored stretch of 30 km (18.6 mi) of empty beach across the sand bar which separates the lake from the sea.

Odisha Tourism Development Corporation

The Odisha Tourism Development Corporation promotes tourism in the state and operate some of the existing tourist bungalows and transportation fleets in commercial line. OTDC's tourist bungalows are called *panthanivas*.

8

Population and Religion

POPULATION OF ODISHA

Odisha is one of the attractive states of India, located in the eastern coast. It is the 11th biggest in terms of population. Odia is the official and most extensively spoken dialect that is spoken by 33.2 million as per the 2001 Census.

The old kingdom of Kalinga, which was assaulted by the Mauryan sovereign Ashoka in 261 BCE and achieving the Kalinga War, relates with the edges of the modern day Odisha. The present day province of Odisha was set up on 1 April 1936 as a region in British India and included Odia-speaking regions. The state gets in a lot of visitors from all across the world for its unique designs and picturesque views.

Population Of Odisha In 2018

As per the 2011 statistics of India, the aggregate population of Odisha is 41,947,358, of which 21,201,678 are male and 20,745,680 are female.

According to the 2001 India assessment, Kohima had a populace of around 78,584. Guys spoke to 53% of the populace and females 47%. Talking about population, in order to check out the population of Odisha in 2018, we need to have a look at the population of the past 5 years. They are as per the following:

1. 2013 – 43.1 Million

2. 2014 – 43.7 Million

3. 2015 – 44.3 Million

4. 2016 – 44.9 Million

5. 2017 – 45.34 Million

Predicting the 2018 population of Odisha is not easy but we can get the idea after analysing the population from the year 2013 – 17. As we have seen that every year the population increases by approximate 0.448 Million people. Hence, the population of Odisha in 2018 is forecast to be 45.34 Million + 0.448 Million = 45.788 Million. So, the population of Odisha in the year 2018 as per estimated data is 45.788 Million.

Odisha Population 2018 –45.788 Million. (estimated).

Demography Of Odisha

The dominating ethnic group in the state is the Odia individuals and Odia is the official language. Linguistic Minorities are Bengali, Hindi, Urdu and Telegu. Schedules Tribes and Scheduled Castes comprise of 16.53% and 22.13% of its population, constituting 38.66% of its population. A segment of the fundamental tribes are Santhal and Kora. The proficiency rate is around 73%, with 82% of males and 64% of females being educated according to the 2011 evaluation. The extent of people living underneath the poverty line in 1999– 2000 was 47.15%, which is twofold the Indian average of 26.10%.

Population Density And Growth Of Odisha

The population density of the state is 269 persons per square kilometre. In the 2001 Census, its population was assessed to be 3.68 Crore, along these lines it has seen a growth of 13.97% in its population in this decade. Population in the state has been growing on a growth rate of 1.4% yearly.

There has been an impressive increment in the number of Christians in Odisha and accordingly brought about the growing rate of population of the state.

Facts About Odisha :

1. Devotees from around India visit the holy city of Puri to appeal to the Gods and approach acquitting for their wrong deeds.

2. A bit of the conspicuous spots which pulls in a ton of travelers are Bhubaneswar, Puri, Konark and so forth.

3. The Odishi dance is widely acclaimed other than fold dance, for instance, Chhau and Chaiti Ghoda.

4. The craftsmanship of Odisha is popular all over the world. The craftsmanship include, silver filigree, tussar texture works and others.

5. The state was made on first April, 1936 in the midst of the British Period. The establishment day of Odisha, generally called Utkala Dibasa, is commended every year on the primary day of April.

DEMOGRAPHICS

Tribal people of Koraput, Odisha

According to the 2011 census of India, the total population of Odisha is 41,947,358, of which 21,201,678 (50.54%) are male and 20,745,680 (49.46%) are female, or 978 females per 1000 males. This represents a 13.97% increase over the population in 2001. The population density is 269 per km^2.

The dominant ethnic group is the Odia people, and Odia is the official language; it is spoken as a native language by 81.8% of the population. Other minority languages of the state are Hindi, Telugu, Santali, Kui, Urdu, Bengali and Ho. Some of the important tribes are Ho, Santhal, Bonda, Munda, Oraon, Kandha, Mahali and Kora.

The literacy rate is 73%, with 82% of males and 64% of females being literate, according to the 2011 census.

The proportion of people living below the poverty line in 1999–2000 was 47.15% which is nearly double the Indian average of 26.10%.

Data of 1996–2001 showed the life expectancy in the state was 61.64 years, higher than the national value of years. The state has a birth rate of 23.2 per 1,000 people per year, a death rate of 9.1 per 1,000 people per year, an infant mortality rate of 65 per 1000 live birth and a maternal·mortality rate of 358 per 1,000,000 live births. Odisha has a Human Development Index of 0.442 as of 2011.

RELIGION

Religion in Odisha (2011)

Hinduism (93.63%)

Christianity (2.76%)

Islam (2.17%)

Sarnaism (1.14%)

Sikhism (1.05%)

Buddhism (0.03%)

Jainism (0.02%)

The majority (over 94%) of people in the state of Odisha are Hindu and there is also a rich cultural heritage in the state. For example, Odisha is home to several Hindu figures. Sant Bhima Bhoi was a leader of the Mahima sect movement. Sarala Das, a Hindu Khandayat, was the translator of the epic Mahabharata in Odia. Chaitanya Das was a Buddhistic-Vaishnava and writer of the *Nirguna Mahatmya*. Jayadeva was the author of the *Gita Govinda*.

The *Odisha Temple Authorisation Act* of 1948 empowered

the Government of Odisha to have Hindu temples open for all Hindus including the Harijans.

Perhaps the oldest scripture of Odisha is the *Madala Panji* from the Puri Temple believed from 1042 AD. Famous Hindu Odia scripture includes the 16th-century *Bhagabata* of Jagannatha Dasa. In the modern times Madhusudan Rao was a major Odia writer, who was a Brahmo Samajist and shaped modern Odia literature at the start of the 20th century.

Christians in Odisha account for about 2.8% of the population while Odia Muslims account for 2.2% as per census figures of 2001. The Sikh, Buddhist and Jain communities together account for 0.1% of the population

RELIGION OF ODISHA

Orissa is known for its respect and mutual tolerance towards other religions. One can vividly witness how religion in Orissa has evolved from animism, nature worship, shamanism, ancestor worship & fethism to the highly evolved forms of religion like Hinduism, Islam, Christianism, Buddhism and Jainism. However, the religion followed by a major proportion of the population of the state is Hinduism.

Among the states of India, Orissa has perhaps the highest concentration of the Hindus, although all other religions have their followers in it.

In 1971, the Hindus formed 92 per cent of the total population; the Muslims, Christians and Buddhists forming 1.5, 1.7 and .04 per cent respectively. The balance is accounted for by the other religions including the tribal religion of Sarana followed mostly by the Santals. Orissa is a land of religious tolerance and the people belonging to different religions and faiths live harmoniously, often within the same village.

The synthesis & harmony of the different forms of Brahminic worship Vaishnavite, Shaivite, Shakta, Ganapatya are all to be found in the great and grand temple of Jagannath or whose origin goes back to the tribal worship of Wood God. Around him, resolves the entire cultural milieu of Orissa. Religion &

culture cannot be separated in a land, which claims to celebrate thirteen festivals in twelve month.

The most commendable thing about Orissa is that, there is unity in diversity. People belonging to different religions and castes live harmoniously and there is a feeling of brotherhood amongst them.

Even if the most dominant religion in Orissa is Hinduism still Orissa is the second state in India after Bihar, in which Buddhism has flourished a lot. Another religion that has made a great impact on the religious lifestyles of the people of the state is Jainism. The best examples of Jain monuments are the caves of Khandagiri and Udaygiri. The three pilgrimage cities of Bhubaneswar , Puri and Konark are worth a visit if one wants to see the depth of the religious cultural heritage of Orissa.

RELIGIONS IN ODISHA: POPULAR RELIGIONS IN THE HISTORY OF ORISSA

Jainism

Two Jaina works namely Jaina Harivamsa Purana and Harivadriya Vritti tell us that Mahavir himself came to Kalinga to preach his religion in the 6th century B.C. By 4th century B.C. Jaina images were being worshipped in Kalinga. Further, Hatigumpha inscription describes that Nandaraja (Mahapadmananda) took away the image of Kalinga jina from Kalinga. From evidence, it is clear that by the 2nd or 1st century B.C. Jainism Chedi king Kharavela. Dr. K.C. Panigrahi holds that Kharavela brought back the seat of Kalinga jina from Magadha after his victory over Magadha in the 12th year of his reign.

Khandagiri-Udayagiri hills near Bhubaneswar became the great seat of Jainism during the reign of Kharavela. According to the Hatigumpha inscrip-tion Kharavela built 117 caves for the habitation of the Jaina monks. These caves were very simple in design, specifically meant for the austere Jaina monks.

Kharavela himself was a devout Jaina but tolerant towards other faiths.

After Kharavela, his successors Vadukha and Kudepasiri extended their support to the spread of Jainism in Orissa. After the fall of the Chedi kings, the Murunda dynasty which ruled over some parts of Orissa and Bihar also patronized Jainism. A gold coin discovered from Sisupalagarh, about 5 miles from Bhubaneswar mentions the name of a king Dhammadamadhara of Murunda dynasty who was a Jaina by faith, ruled in third century A.D. According to the evidence available in the Asanpat inscription of Keonjhar, the Bhanja king Satrunjaya patronized Jaina monks (mentioned as Nirgranthas) in his capital.

The imperial Gupta extended their full support to the spread of Jainism in the length and breadth of Orissa. Jainism continued to remain a supreme religion along with Buddhism, Saivism and Brahminical religion. Hiuen Tsang in his accounts said that during his visit to Orissa in 639 A.D., he saw 10,000 Jaina (Tirlhika) monks in the Kangoda territory. The Banapur Copper plate of Dharmaraja of Sailodbhava dynasty reveals that he donated some lands to a Jaina monk Prabudha Chandra. Jainism remained supreme till 11th century A. D. as has been proved from the discovery of Jaina images from various places of Orissa.

A number of Jaina images have been found in different parts of Jaipur. The images of Parsanatha and Chandranath have been discovered from near Jaipur which further speak that the Bhaumakara Kings also patronized this religion. The Jaina images found near Podasingidi in the Keonjhar district indicate that in the 8th century A.D., this place was a great centre of Jainism. In the Prachi Valley, Jainism flourished to a great extent during the Bhaumakara period which has been proved by the presence of Rishavanatha surrounded by other Tirthankaras in the Swapneswara temple.

During the Somavamsi rule, Udyata Keshari built some caves in the Khandagiri hills in the 11th century A.D. Thus, it is very evident that from the time of Kharavela till the Somavamsi rule Khandagiri-Udayagiri hills remained as a great centre of Jainism. During this period, a type of synthesis between Saivism and Jainism appears to have taken place in the Mukteswara temple through the carving of Jaina images on the temple (Siva temple).

Budhism

The Mahaparinirvana Sutta states that Kalinga was one of the kingdoms to have obtained the tooth relic of Budha after his cremation at Kusinar. This sacred tooth relic was enshrined and worshipped at Dantapur, the capital of Kalinga. Asoka's conversion to Buddhism after the Kalinga was in 261 B.C. gave tremendous impetus to Buddhism to Kalinga. The Asokan edicts at Dhauli and Jaugada spear about the welfare activities of emperor Asoka. Dr. K.C. Panigrahi maintains that the Sivalinga of Bhaskareswar temple was originally an Asokan pillar. He further says that the elephant which is found at Dauli is a sacred Buddhist symbol.

By the time of Asoka, three schools of thoughts on Buddhism had emerged such as Theravadin, Savarstivadin, and Mahasanghamika. Asoka belonged to the first group. He built a monastery for the Theravadin monk Tissa who happened to be his own brother, at Bhojakagiri in Kalinga. After Asoka, the Sarvastivadin school of Buddhism flourished to a maximum degree.

From the earliest time up to 7th century A.D., both Hinayan and Mahayan schools were prevalent in Orissa. Hiuen Tsang narrates that there continued the controversy between these schools of thought in Odradesa. At that time to avoid the conflict Harsha Vardhan requested Silabhadra, the Chancellor of Nalanda University to send some Mahayan scholars for holding a conference with the Hinayan Monks of Odra.

By the end of sixth century A.D., a number of Buddhist centres had developed in Orissa. The Birupa-Chitrotpala Valley in Cuttack district, Jaipur on the bank of Baitarani river and Jayrampur in Balasore district were the important centres of Buddhism. In the Buddhist monasteries at Ratnagiri, Lalitgiri, and Udayagiri in the Birupa-Chitrotpala Valley we find archaeological remains. The great Buddhist Vihar about which Hiuen Tsang men-tions in his accounts probably is located in this famous valley. According to his description, Mahayan Buddhism was predominant in the Odra country.

By the end of 7th century A.D. Tantrik or Vijrayan Buddhism began to have a grip over Orissa. In course of time, Orissa became a centre of Tantrik Buddhism. The Tantrik Buddhism got royal patronage from the Bhaumakar rulers like Kshemakardeva, Sivakardeva I and Suvakardeva I who assumed the Buddhist titles like Paramopasaka, Paramatathagata and Parama Saugata, etc.

According to the Tibetan historian Taranath, Rahula was born in Odivisa (Orissa). He became the Chancellor of the Nalanda University early in 9th century A.D. The Tantrik Buddhist images such as Marichi, Lokesvara, Tara and Jambhala have been discovered from Ayodhya in the Nilgiri sub-division of the Balasore district.

The site of Viratagarh near Khiching in Mayurbhanj district also clearly speaks about the spread of Tantrik form of Buddhism in many parts of Orissa. According to some scholars, Tantrik Buddhism was not confined to Orissa but also in the whole Eastern India covering Bengal, Bihar, Assam and Orissa.

Buddhism received royal patronage during Bhaumakara rule in Orissa. The character of Buddhism underwent substantial changes during the Bhaumakara rule. The Somavamsi rulers were followers of Saivism and thus did not patronize Buddhism. Nevertheless Buddhism continued to prevail even up to the Ganga period.

Saivism

Saivism is an ancient religious belief in India. It had its origin in the Indus Valley civilization. In Orissa, the worship of Siva appears to have been introduced by the Kushanas. The coins of some Kushana kings, who were ruling in the second century A. D. have been discovered from the Sisupalagarh. These coins bear the image of Siva. Again coins discovered from the Mayurbhanj and Keonjhar region gives us the earliest iconic evidence of the Siva worship. The Natraj image of Siva found in Asanpat in Keonjhar district is a naked Urddhavalirna form of Siva with eight hands. This image depicts the Tandava dance of Lord Siva.

In the Gupta period, Saivism occupied a significant place in the religious life of the people of Orissa. The Eastern Gangas who established their rule in Kalinga naturally patronized the spread of Saivism in Orissa. During this period, Saivism triumphed over Buddhism. Caves were built near Bhaskaresvara Siva temple in Bhubaneswar for the habitation of Saiva ascetics.

According to the evidence found in Ekamra Purana, Saivism appears to have acquired greater grip over Buddhism. The Sailodbhavas were great Saivites. The Siva temples of Parsuramesvara, Satrughnesvara, Bharatesvara, Lakshmanesvara and Swarnejalesvara in Bhubaneswar were built by the Sailodbhava rulers. Dr. K.C. Panigrahi maintains that Sasanka of Gauda (Bengal), the great Saivite erected the Tribhubanesvara temple for Lord Siva in Bhubaneswara. Probably the name Bhubaneswar has been derived from the name of this temple.

The Bhaumakara kings built a number of Siva temples in Bhubaneswar. They claimed themselves as great devotees of Siva and claimed the titles of Parama Mahesvara. The Bhaumakara kings and queens donated lands for the Siva temples. The Bhauma rulers reflected their religious ideas in the temple sculpture. Dr. Panjgrahi holds that the Lakulisa images are the modified images of Buddha in Dharmachakra Pravartan mudra. In the tantrik vaital temple where the main deity is Chamunda the Saivite image of Lakulisa and the Buddhist image of Amoghasiddhi are to be found.

Saivism reached to the height of its glory in Orissa during the Somavamsi rule. They claimed the titles of Mahasivagupta and Parama Maheswara etc. They introduced a new text on Saivism in the coastal Orissa in 11th century A.D. This new sect is called Mathamayura sect which was found in Kosala region where from the Somavamsi rulers came. In the Rajarani temple built by Indraratha, a Mattamayura Siva image called Jatamukta wearing a garland of skulls is found. The erection of the Lingaraj temple by Yayati II is a clear evidence of the influence of Saivism on the Somavamsi rulers.

Saivism and Vaisnavism developed side by side in Orissa. The co-existence of these two religious cults has been attested by the worship of the deity of Hari (Vishnu) and Hara (Siva) in the temple of Lingaraj. This conception of Harihara worship continued to influence the people of Orissa throughout the period of Ganga and Suryavamsi rule in Orissa.

Vaishnavism

The worship of Vishnu in Orissa can be traced back to the Mathar period who ruled over Kalinga in the fourth-fifth centuries A.D. The Mathar kings were devotees of Vishnu and built a temple on the Mahendra Mountain to worship the deity. A Vishnu image of Mathar period bearing conch and wheel is found on the bank of the Vindusarovar tank in front of the Ananta Vashudeva temple at Bhubaneswar. The Mathar kings popularized the wor-ship of Vishnu in the coastal region of Orissa.

During the Sailodbhava rule, the influence of Vishnu worship gradually declined as the kings were basically Saivites. No doubt Saivism enjoyed a predominant position from the post-Mathar period down to the end of the Somavamsi rule, yet Vaishnavism did not suffer much. The Sailodbhava rulers expressed some leniency towards Vaishnavism. The temples of Sailodbhava period contain Siva as the main deity but on the walls of the temples some sculptural representation of the image of Vishnu are main-tained.

During the Bhaumakara rule, Vaishnavism continued to remain as an ancillary cult of Saivism. The image of Harihara in Vaital temple is a clear example of this. The Bhaumakara queen Tribhuban Mahadevi was a Parama Vaishnavi, (devotee of Vishnu).

The Somavamsi rulers conceived the idea of Vishnu worship along with the images of Siva which is found in the Lingaraj temple. The representation of Nanda, Yasoda and Child Krishna in the temple is a clear evidence of the attitude of the Somavamsi kings of Orissa. Towards the close of their rule, they patronized Vaishnavism and it was rising rapidly to prominence.

Chodagangadeva, the founder of the imperial Ganga rule in Orissa patronized Vaishnavism soon after the establishment of his supremacy over Utkal in the early 12th Century A.D. This is evident from the visit of the great Vaishnava saint of the south Ramanujacharya to Puri. Chodagangadeva himself claimed as Parama Vaishnava and erected the magnificent temple for Purushotama-Narayan at Puri.

Jayadeva popularized the cult of Vishnu in Orissa through his Gitagovinda. He introduced the cult of Krishna and his female consort Radha. He advocated the concept of ten incarnations of Vishnu (Dasha avatar) from Fish (Mina to Kalki) Narahari Tirtha, the deciple of Ananda Tirtha who was the founder of dvaita or dualistic philosophy of Vishnu. Bhanudeva I caused the construction of Ananta Vasudeva temple for Vishnu in Bhubaneswar which was completed by Chandrikadevi, the daughter of Anangavimadeva III. Thus, the construction of the Vishnu temple in the centre of Saivism is a clear evidence of the ascendency of Vaisnavism in the 13th Century A.D. The representation of the image of Rama, Lakshmana, Sita, Hanuman, Krishna and Gopis in the sculptures of Ananta Vasudeva temple speaks of a change of the idea of worship of Vishnu.

Of the ten incarnations of Vishnu, Nrusimha became very popular during the reign of early Ganga rules. The construction of the Sun temple at Konark testifies the worship of Vishnu in solar aspect. The popular concept of Radha and Gopi and their sexual orgies with Krishna also had its beginning during the Ganga period.

Vaishnavism continued to remain as the most important religion with an impressive influence on the people in Orissa from 12th Century A.D. onwards. Srikshetra Puri attracted many Vaishnava saints including Srichaitanya of Bengal in the early part of 16th Century A.D. Vaishnavism propounded by Srichaitanya are known as Gaudiya form of Vaishnavism.

In Orissa, the five eminent poets known as panchasakha—Jagannath, Balarama, Achyutananda, Yasovanta and Ananta—professed about the shunya or void in their works. Orissa form of Vaishnavism centred round the worship of Jagannath and gave less importance to Krishna, the lover of Gopis.

By the beginning of the 16th Century A.D., Vaishnavism became a challenge to Brahmnism. It worked as a popular socio-religious movement throughout Orissa. The Suryavamsi rulers patronised Vaishnavism to a great extent and surrendered themselves as the Sevakas before Lord Jagannath. The spread of this religion also could be possible through other literary works.

The religious drama Jagannath-Vallava written by Ray Ramananda, the Governor of Rajahmundri during the reign of Prataprudradeva had profound influence on the people of Orissa. He in the drama depicted the premabhakti, the divine love of the Gopis for Lord Krishna. Thus, Vaishnavism either in Orissan form or in Bengal form roused the religious devotion among all sections of the society irrespective of caste and creed in Orissa.

Jagannath Cult

The origin of Lord Jagannath, the most important deity of Puri, around whom the religious life of the people of Orissa evolved since a long time past has been shrouded in mystery. Some scholars hold that Jagannath was originally a tribal deity. Dr. Anncharlott Eschmann maintains that the Navakalevar periodical renewal of wooden deity ritual is a tribal custom.

The legends regarding the origin of Lord Jagannath has been described by Sarala Das in his Mahabharata. Further in Deula Tola of Nilambar Das, Skanda Purana, Brahma Purana, and Padma Purana, etc., it has been described that the deity of Lord Jagannath had the tribal and Brahmanical link in the initial stage. According to Sarala Das, the dead body of Lord Krishna transformed into wooden form, landed at the Puri sea shore, Jara Sabar picked it up and worshipped it.

Subsequently, Indradyumna, the Somavamsi King, got three wooden images made out of the log and built the temple for the deities Jagannath, Balabhadra and Devi Subhadra. Nilambar Das in his Deula Tola says that Indradyumna, the King of Malava, got a piece of sacred wood which was the metamorphosed shape of Nilamadhaba of the Sabar Chief Visvavasu and out of that sacred, wood he made three images. Both these narrations speak of the Vaishnavite origin of Lord Jagannath.

Some scholars hold the Buddhist origin of the trinity of Jagannath. It is said by them that the tooth relic of Buddha is preserved in the image of Jagannath. They further say that Snana Yatra (Bathing festival of the deities), Ratha Yatra (Car festival) and the sharing of Kaibalya (sacred food) on equal footing by all castes are of Buddhist origin.

It is generally accepted by many scholars that Jagannath in the earliest phase was known as Purushottama. Vamana Parana of 7th century A.D. refers Purushottama as Vishnu. The presiding deity of Puri was known as Purushottama which is one of the thousand incarnations of Vishnu. Some scholars are of the opinion that Purushottama though an epithet of Vishnu has tantrik significance.

It represents the erotic aspect of Vishnu, when Purushottama is found with his erotic partner Lakshmi. Jayadeva in his Gitagovinda also with the erotic sports of Krishna with Radha and identified Radha with Kamala or Lakshmi. Such was the nature of the cult of Purushottama-Jagannath in Orissa which compelled Chodagangadeva to have caused the construction of the temple in Puri. The Ganga period recognised the deity Jagannath as the patron deity. Anangabhimadeva III went to the point of telling his empire as Purushottam Samraya.

During the reign of Suryavamsi Gajapatic Kapilendra, he used the name of Jagannath in the day-to-day administration of his empire. He used to obtain prior permission of the deity before committing anything in administration. Purushottamadeva, the successor of Kapilendradeva, com-posed Abhinava Gitagovinda glorifying the name of Lord Jagannath. During the reign of Prataprudradeva Chaitanya completed the whole process of identification of Jagannath with Krishna.

Jagannath cult, however, has tremendous influence over the social, religious and political life of the people of Orissa. Jagannath cult, no doubt, assimilates different religious cults like tribal religion, Brahmanism, Buddhism, Saivism, Saktism, Tantricism and Vaishnavism into one religious cult which everybody accepts.

Sakti Cult

The worship of defied form of female energy known as Sakti is traced back to the Indus Valley Civilization. In Orissa, the worship of this Sakti is found at Jajpur in the form of Viraja from very ancient time. Harivamsa, Vayupurana and Mahabharata refer the worship of Viraja at Jajpur. But for some time, Sakti worship was overshadowed by the influence of Buddhism.

The influence of Brahmanical religion during Gupta period re-established the power and energy of this female image known as Sakti at Jajpur. The present image, of Viraja in the temple of Jajpur belongs to the 5th century A.D. This, image also called Mahisamardini, is a two handed Durga engaged in killing Mahisasura or the buffalo demon. This is, thus, the earliest form of Goddess Durga. Besides Jajpur, the image of this type is also found at Somesvar near Kakatpur in the Prachi Valley.

During the Bhaumakar rule, the image of Durga became eight-armed. Subsequently, this image became ten-armed towards the later part of the Bhaumakar. The Dasabhuja (ten-armed) Durga was depicted at that time as the war Goddess armed with the weapons of different Gods. Though the early Bhaumakara Kings were the followers of Buddhism, yet Sakti worship flourished at Jajpur, their capital. The popularity of this image at Jajpur is due to the fact that the Bhaumakara queen Tribhuvan Mahadevi compared herself with Katyayini.

Tantricism influenced the worship of the mother Goddess from 7th century A.D. onwards. The Tantriks worshipped the mother Goddess as the source of power and energy. The Buddhist Tantricism called Vajrayan conceived the idea of Goddess worship which is evident from the presence of Tara image in such places as Banpur Vanesvaranasi, Ratnagiri and Khiching, the places having Buddhist importance.

The Bhaumakara Kings patronized Sakti worship. The Tantrik-Sakti worship dominated Bhubaneswar, an important centre of Saivism. The Kapalikas who were the devotees of Siva, worshipped the goddess Chamunda and Mahisamardini to get their Siddis. For this reason, four Sakti shrines were erected on four sides of Vindu Sarovar tank near the Lingaraj temple.

Of these temples Vaitala occupies an important place. The deity of this temple is Chamunda and the Tantrik rites like human or animal sacrifice were being practiced. The Sakti worshippers of the Bhaumakara period conceived the idea of worshipping a group of seven mother Goddesses called Saptamatruka (Varahi, Indrani, Vaishnavi, Kaumari, Sivani, Brahmi and Chamunda).

The Tantricism of the Brahmanical society developed into a Yogini cult in Orissa. Kalika Purana indicates that Yogini cult had its origin in Orissa. Kapalikas were the devotees of Siva and Yoginis were the devotees of Sakti or Durga. The Yogini temples scattered throughout Orissa contain Sakti the defied form of female energy in different manifestations of Sakti.

The Yogini temple of Hirapur near Bhubaneswar is presided by Mahamaya, a ten armed Goddess. The principal deity of the Yogini temple at Ranipur-Jharial in Bolangir district is a terrific Chamunda. As this temple is situated in the territory of the Somavamsis of Kosala, it is very clear that Somavamsi rulers did not put any restriction on the worship of Sakti.

No doubt, the Somavamsis were Saivites yet workship of Sakti or Tantricism did not suffer from any antipathy from the rulers because of the close relationship between Saivism and Sakti worship. The cult of Siva is known as Bhairava and that of the Sakti is known as Bhairavi, Parvati, Mahamaya and Durga. Chodagangadeva was very much against Sakti worship but the worship of Goddess Durga did not disappear from Orissa.

The Gangas caused the construction of the temple of Parvati inside the Lingaraj temple compound. They also built the temples of Lakshmi and Vimala inside the compound of the Jagannath temple. The Bala Avakas of Balaram Das tells us that Lord Jagannath is attended by 64 Yoginis, Katyayini, Saptamatruka, Vimala and Viraja.

The very concept of Sakti worship along with the cult of Jagannath and Vaisnavism could be adjusted within the deities of Srikshetra during the Ganga and Somavamsi rule. The image of Devi Subhadra along with Lord Jagannath and Balabhadra clearly indicates that the Sakti cult became a common concept among the people which continued to dominate in different parts of Orissa in different names.

Islam

The Muslim rule in Orissa resulted in the Immigration of Muslim officials from different parts of India. From the very beginning of their rule the rulers tried to raise Muslim monuments on the foundation of some Hindu monuments built earlier. Propagation of Islam became the main objectives of all Muslim rulers. Consequent upon this, a number of Muslim mosques were built in such places at Cuttack, Jajpur, Kendrapara and Balasore.

Zuma Masjid of Balubazar in Cuttack is regarded as the best of Muslim monuments in Orissa. The coming of the Muslims into Orissa at a later period became responsible for the survival of many Hindu monuments in this country. This is also a reason for the comparatively small percentage of Muslim population in Orissa.

Muslim rule in Orissa to a great extent hampered the freedom of religious activities among the Hindu community. Pilgrim tax was imposed on every pilgrim coming to Puri. This came into force probably during the reign of Aurangzeb. At various points, the worship of Lord Jagannath was restricted by Muslim rulers.

In course of time, a synthesis of Hindu-Muslim unity could be possible in Orissa during the Mughal period beginning from the time of Akbar—the Great Salabeg, a Muslim, became a beloved devotee of Lord Jagannath. Satyapir became a common deity of worship to both Hindus and Muslims.

Many Sataypir deities were established in many parts of Orissa, of which the Satyapira of Kaipadar is famous. Thus, Pira worship in every household particularly at the time of birth of a child symbolizes the unity among Hindus and Muslims during the Mughal period.

The religious temperament of the people brought about a social change Mughal Tamsha of Bhadrakh is the influence of Hindu-Muslim unity which developed into a social system on special occasions to which the people of Orissa gave their approval. As in other parts of India, Orissa did not suffer much in this regard. No doubt monuments, deities were demolished by Kalapahara an iconoclast yet Hindu-Muslim unity could exist in Orissa.

Mahima Cult

In the second half of 19th century when educated urban elite were forced to accept Brahmo faith as a reaction to the activities of the Christian missionaries, "Mahima dharma" checked the process of mass conversion into Christianity. This indigenous cult brought a large number of uneducated rural people into its fold. Gradually this cult spread to the neighbouring states like Bengal, Assam, Andhra Pradesh and Madhya Pradesh, etc.

The founder of this new cult could not come to limelight and, thus, the activities were shrouded in obscurity for a pretty long time. In course of time, this belief was changed and the philosophy and teachings of Mahima Gosaim was understood in proper perspective.

Mahima Gosaim appeared for the first time at Puri in 1826. It is said that during that period, he was virtually sleeping on the Jagannath road without uttering any sound. He had only saffron coloured Kaupina as his belongings. From Puri, he travelled to nearby places and passing through Bhubaneswar and Cuttack, he reached on the top of the Kapilas hills in 1838.

There he gave up clothes and began to wear the bulk of Kumbhi tree, lie attained the perfection and started preaching his ideas among his relatives and friends. Siddha Govinda Baba met him on the hill and was initiated into this cult. Bhagirathi Bhramarabar, the Raja of Dhenkanal, became his devotee and thus patronised the cult in 1862.

Mahima Gosaim, coming down from the hill, entered into the plains to propagate his new cult which gradually became a very popular religious cult among the people of Orissa. He died in 1876. His mortal remains were buried at Joranda in Dhenkanal.

In Mahima cult, Param Brahma the absolute reality is said to be Alekha (without description), Anakar (without any shape) and Anadi (without end). That power is indescribable beyond all categories of thought. Mayabada of Sankar has no place in Mahima cult. Mahimavada is claimed to be pure and logical. Visuddhadvaitavada is the main cardinal principle of this cult.

The philosophy of Mahima cult in not incompatible to the teachings of Vedas and Upanishad. The authenticity of Veda was not rejected by Mahima dharma. It made an attempt to reform Hinduism from within. Mahima Gosaim vehemently criticized idolatry and caste system and tried his utmost to remove the remote possibility of idol worship.

In this process, he declared that worship is due only to the Guru who is Param brahama but not to any individual. Mahimadharma discouraged caste system and allowed inter-dining system. He disallowed his disciples to worship him. Thus, he strongly rejected the evils of the society.

The followers of Mahima cult were required to travel constantly to collect only one meal a day from any house-holder irrespective of any caste or creed. They were also restricted not to stay more than one night in one village. Mahima dharma allowed only male devotees to the monastic order only to maintain purity of mind in this cult.

Mahima Gosaim, by his long missionary career, had laid down strong foundations for his new cult. He, through his soft words attracted the people in large number. He had propagated this new cult not only in the coastal districts but also in the hilly tracts of Garhjats of Orissa.

He had profound influence on the people of the neighbouring provinces Many ashrams were established on the patronage of the ruling chiefs of Orissa. The important ashram of the cult in Western Orissa was established by philospher-poet Bhima Bhoi at Khaliapali on the bank of Ang river.

The devotional songs of Bhima Bhoi helped much to popularize the new cult among the common people of Orissa. By the second half of 19th century, Mahima cult grew into a popular religion in Orissa which could counteract the movements of the Christian Missionaries and the anglicised Brahmo movement.

Mahima cult generated a ray of new hope among the millions of Hindus who could aspire to find salvation in their own traditional system but in a simple way. In this process, there was no fear of any rituals and the predominance of the priests.

Thus, in the caste ridden society of Orissa in 19th century, it emerged as a revolutionary cult which said that all men and women could take refuge in Alekh Param Brahma. The aim and objective of Mahima Gosaim to liberate the downtrodden men and women from the bondage of caste, superstitious beliefs and traditions, ritualistic idolatry and predominance of priest could be materialized into action in Orissa. The idea of one Godhood seems to be ideal which he propounded thus brought about tremendous influence on the religious, social and cultural life of the people.

Christianity

Missionary activities preaching against idolatry in general and worship in particular stated in Orissa in 1823. The Baptist Missionary Society undertook the work at Puri in the right earnest against the worship of Lord Jagannath (Lord of the Universe) which attracts the stream of people from every nook and comer of India.

Besides the specific attention of the missionaries against the influence of Jagannath cult, they undertook their usual activities of preaching the gospels of Christianity and distributing the Bible and other religious pam-phlets. They aimed at destroying out age-old belief in traditional faith and institutions by converting many into Christianity.

But for first six years, they could not convert a single man from the province. The first Oriya convert was Gangadhar Sarangi, a Brahmin and gradually more Oriya accepted this new faith. Baptists converted as many as 540 Oriyas by 1850 which went up to 1,629 in 1871.

A group of Oriya mostly disciples of an ashram founded by Sadhu Sundar Das at Kajibar in Cuttack districts accepted Christianity.

The dis-ciples read the missionary pamphlets and developed much interest in the new faith. Sadhu Sundar Das was a great reformist guru who did not believe in traditional Hindu belief. The missionaries met the Guru and his disciples in October 1826 which ultimately led the disciples to embrace Christianity.

The Oriya converts became evangelists and engaged in preaching different parts of the province. Several missionary settlements sprang up in Cuttack, Balasore, Jaleswar, Ganjam and Sambalpur. By 1835, the American missionaries were associated with the evangelical works in Orissa. For a pretty long time Sambalpur turned to be the centre of operation. Subsequently, they settled at Balasore.

The missionaries became busy to mobilise the people about their religion through Jananaruna the Oriya journal. Large number of Oriya books for vernacular schools were written and printed by them. These efforts in the field of education influenced the Government to follow an effective educational policy and encouraged the people to imbibe a new spirit in the caste ridden Hindu society.

The missionaries also opened new prospects in philanthropic activities during the period of natural calamities in Orissa, a province which invariably suffered from the seasonal calamities. A number of orphanages were opened for both boys and girls. The destitute were provided with food, shelter and vocational education to earn their subsistence. Consequent upon these activi-ties, many orphan boys and girls accepted the new creed.

The missionaries thus created a new atmosphere and roused the minds of the people to face such challenges of the society. They could realise the realities of life. The early Christian converts formed a small exclusive community without social influence or leadership. Many factors like lack of good communication, slow growth of English education, rigidity of social customs and traditions hindered Christianity to make headway in Orissa. Orissa remained uncongenial a land for the growth of the new faith.

However, many Oriyas in course of time embraced Christianity with the hope of getting Government jobs with lucrative salaries and accumulated wealth and power. Very slowly the situation changed. Critical self analysis by thoughtful Hindus inaugurated a new outlook for socio-religious movement in Orissa.

The anglicised Brahmo movement of Bengal influenced terribly the people in the sixties of the 19th century. Thus, Christianity brought about a new social change even though not up to the expectations of the ruling community in the first half of the 19th century which some way or other changed in the second half of the last century. In the early part of the 20th century, the missionaries could penetrate into tribal areas where they could sustain comfortably.

Thus, the educated middle class intelligentsia mass in the second half of the 19th century mostly inclined towards Christianity. However, it was confined to them only as they did not venture to peruse others to accept the new faith hastily.

9

Art, Architecture, Fair and Festivals

ARTS OF ODISHA

The Indian state of Odisha has a rich cultural and artistic heritage. Due to the reign of many different rulers in the past, arts and crafts in Odisha underwent many changes giving an artistic diversity today in the forms of traditional handicrafts, painting and carving, dance and music.

Dance and music

Odissi dance

Odissi dance is particularly prominent and in itself displays the fusion of many styles in history. Odissi is one of the eight classical dance forms of India. The classic treatise of Indian dance, Natya Shastra, refers to it as Odra-Magadhi. 1st century BCE bas-reliefs in the hills of Udaygiri (near god hanuman) testify to its antiquity. It was suppressed under the British Raj but has been reconstructed since India gained independence.

It is particing distinguished from other classical Indian dance forms by the importance it places upon the tribhangi (literally: three parts break), the independent movement of head, chest and pelvis, and upon the basic square stance known as chauka. There are a number of musical instruments used to accompany the Odissi dance, including the pakhawaj (also known as the madal), the bansuri (bamboo flute), the manjira (metal cymbals), the sitar and the tanpura.

The Odissi tradition existed in three schools; *Mahari, Nartaki,* and *Gotipua.* Maharis were Odishan devadasis or temple girls (their name deriving from *Maha* (great) and *Nari* or *Mahri* (chosen) particularly those at the temple of Jagganath at Puri. Early Maharis performed mainly nritta (pure dance) and abhinaya (interpretation of poetry) based on mantras & slokas, later Maharis, especially, performed dance sequences based on the lyrics of Jayadev's Gita Govinda. *Bhitari gauni Maharis,* were allowed in the inner temple while *bahari gauni Maharis,* though in the temples, were excluded from the *sanctum sanctorum.*

A dancer portrays Radha suffering over the infidelity of sri Krishna.

By the 6th century the Gotipua tradition was emerging. One of the reasons given for the emergence of Gotipuas is that Vaishnavas did not approve of dancing by women. Gotipuas were young boys dressed as girls and taught the dance by the Maharis. During this period, Vaishnava poets composed innumerable lyrics in Odia dedicated to Radha and Krishna. Gotipuas danced to these compositions. The Gotipuas stepped out of the precincts of the temples.

The Nartaki dance took place in the royal courts, where it was much cultivated before the British period. At that time the misuse of devadasis came under strong attack, so that Odissi dance withered in the temples and became unfashionable at court. Only the remnants of the gotipua school remained, and the reconstruction of the style required an archaeological and anthropological effort that has tended to foster a conservative purism.

Others

Stone carving, Konark Sun Temple

Aside from the Odissi dance there are many other forms of dance and folk performances in Odisha. These include Baunsa Rani, Chaiti Ghoda, Changu Nata, Chhau, Dalkhai, Danda Nata, Dasakathia, Dhanu Jatra, Ghanta Patua, Ghoomra, Jhoomar, Karma, Kathinacha, Kedu, Kela Keluni, Krishna Leela, Medha Nacha, Naga Dance, Paika Nrutya, Pala, Patua Jatra, Puppet Dance, Rama Leela, Ranappa and Samprada.

Music

The 16th century witnessed the compilation of literature within music. The four important treatises written during that time are Sangitamava Chandrika, Natya Manorama, Sangita Kalalata and Gita Prakasha. Orissi music is a combination of four distinctive kinds of music, namely, Chitrapada,

Dhruvapada, Panchal and Chitrakala. When music uses artwork, it is known as Chitikala. A unique feature of Oriya music is the Padi, which consists of singing of words in fast beat.

Orissi music is more two thousand five hundred years old and comprises a number of categories. Of these, the five broad ones are Tribal Music, Folk Music, Light Music, Light-Classical Music and Classical Music. Anyone who is trying to understand the culture of Odisha must take into account its music, which essentially forms a part of its legacy.

In the ancient times, there were saint-poets who wrote the lyrics of poems and songs that were sung to rouse the religious feelings of people. It was by the 11th century that the music of Odisha, in the form of Triswari, Chatuhswari, and Panchaswari, underwent transformation and was converted into the classical style.

Handicrafts

Major handicrafts in Odisha include applique work, brass and bell metal, silver filigree and stone carving. Other forms include Lacquer, Papier Mache, and tribal combs, handlooms and wood and traditional stone carving.

Painting

The history of painting in Odisha dated back to ancient times with rock-shelter paintings, some which are dated to the early historic period (300BC-100AD). Apart from the rock painting sites there are several drawings and etching resembling figures on rock surfaces at Digapahandi and Berhampur in Ganjam district and other places. Many of the cave paintings are tribal and rock shelter painting has continued through the centuries as an Oriya tradition. They are often of a decorative nature mixed with rituals and may contain several motifs. Mural paintings in Odisha as elsewhere in India was an ancient tradition and evidence of mural pigment coatings have been found in the caves of Khandagiri and Udayagiri dating back to the reign of Emperor Kharavela who ruled in the 1st century

B.C. On the ceiling of Ravanachhaya at Sitabinji in Keonjhar district is a mural belonging to later Gupta period and shows resemblance to those of the Ajantastyle. From the period of 1600 to present murals were painted in the numerous templates of Odisha depicting sacred figures such as the painting of Buddha Vijaya in the Jagamohana of Lakshmi Temple and inside the Jagannath Temple at Puri, the Biranchinarayana Temple, in Buguda, Ganjam district and so on.

Erotic sculpture in Mukteswar Temple

Pata painting is considered an important form of Oriya painting which originated from the temple of Jagannath at Puri in the 12th century. This style developed under the patronage of the Ganga kings, and the kings of Bhoi dynasty. The purpose of the pata painting was to popularise the cult of Jagannath to the millions of pilgrims visiting Puri. The pata paintings however may take a number of forms and may range from masks to even toys and models.

Structural art

The Jagannatha Temple in Puri, is also known for its applique artwork of Pipili, silver filigree ornamental works from Cuttack, the *Pattachitras* (palm leaf paintings), famous stone utensils of Nilgiri (Balasore) and various tribal influenced cultures. The Sun temple at Konark is famous for its architectural splendour while the 'Sambalpuri textiles', especially the Sambalpuri Saree, equals it in its artistic grandeur. The different colors and varieties of sarees in Odisha make them very popular among the women of the state. The handloom sarees available in Odisha can be of four major types; these are Ikat, Bandha, Bomkai and Pasapalli. Odisha sarees are also available in other colors like cream, maroon, brown and rust. The tie-and-dye technique used by the weavers of Odisha to create motifs on these sarees is unique to this region. This technique also gives the sarees of Odisha an identity of their own.

Sand Art

In Odisha, sand art unique type of art form is developed in Puri.

KALINGA ARCHITECTURE

The Kaliinga architectural style is a style of Hindu architecture which flourished in the ancient Kalinga region or present eastern Indian state of Odisha, West Bengal and northeastern Andhra Pradesh. The style consists of three distinct types of temples: Rekha Deula, Pidha Deula and Khakhara Deula.

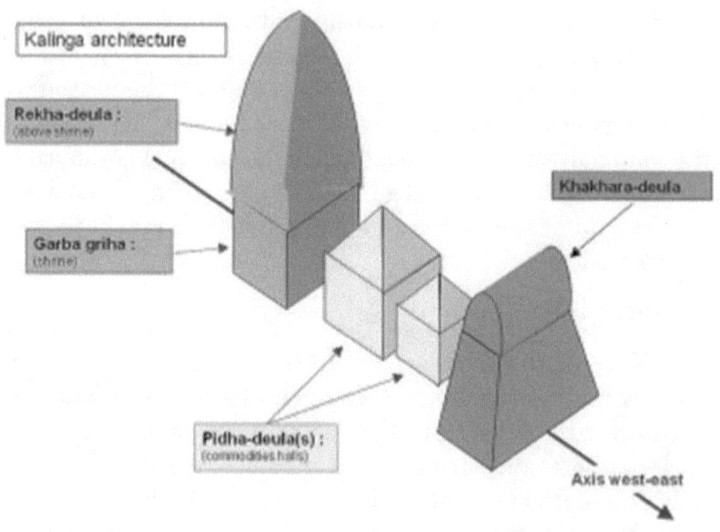

Simplified schema of a Kalinga architecture temple

The Lingaraja Temple, a revered pilgrimage center and the culminating result of the architectural tradition at Bhubaneswar, sixth century AD.

The Jagannath Temple, one of the four holiest places (Dhamas) of Hinduism, in the coastal town of Puriin Odisha.

The former two are associated with Vishnu, Surya and Shiva temples while the third is mainly with Chamunda and Durga temples. The Rekha Deula and Khakhara Deula houses the sanctum sanctorum while the Pidha Deula constitutes outer dancing and offering halls.

In Kalinga, the ancient land of Sakta cult, divine iconography existed since the mythological era. Present day research implies that idols (deities) were placed under auspicious Trees in the ancient days. And maybe today a Temple in general carries various minute details and the overall shape of some heritage tree. The various aspects of a typical Kalinga Temple include Architectural stipulations, Iconography, historical connotations and honoring the traditions, customs and associated legends.

Architecture

Selecting people

According to Manusmti there is a specific hierarchy of

Command for the management of people involved in they are classified as:

1. Kartâ : The Chief patron of the temple, generally the king of the state is designated as kartâ. Hence these devotional ancient architectures often reflect various socio-cultural aspects of society of the time.

2. Mukhya Sthapati : The Chief Architect, The master of the Shilpa Shastras, Vastu Shastra, Dharma Shastra, Agni Purana and Mathematical Calculations. Besides being a very knowledgeable person he is also a very pious man. He translates the Kartâ's vision into an architectural design based on stipulations.

3. Sutra GrahaG□i : The Chief Engineer (can be equated) as he is the person who translates the architecture into actual geometrical dimensions. He is equally proficient in all the required knowledge and most often is the son of the Mukhya Sthapati.

4. Bârdhanikas : The masons, the stone setters

5. Takc□aka : The sculptor with hands that create poetry in stone does all the magnificent carvings and engravings of various forms that has left us spell bound.

Besides these primary set of specialists, various supportive functions are carried out by other people.

Site Selection

Various aspects like type of soil, shape of the Plot, location of the plot, availability and type of space and ground water level, etc. are taken into consideration while selecting the site. Color, density, composition and moisture content of the soil discriminates between the best, middle, sub-middle and worst kind of soil. Based on Vastu Shastra, a rectangular, square, elliptical or circular plot of land is selected in order of preference.

Scale Model

The Mukhya Sthaptya (Main Sculptor similar to Chief Architect) creates a scale model based on traditional stipulations and takes the Karta's (producer / financier) approval. In many instances we see such depictions on walls and motifs.

THE TEMPLE ARCHITECTURE

Architecture in Odisha found its supreme expression in the form of temples, some of which are among, finest in the country. Of these, three are most famous the Lingaraja temple at Bhubaneswar (11th century), the Jagannath Temple at Puri (12th century) and the great Sun Temple at Konark (13th century). These mark the culmination of a distinct style of architecture called the Kalinga style remarkable in its plan elevation and details of decoration. In the simplest form, a temple of this style consists of a structural due, the main temple or shrine and the frontal porch.

While the main temple, called Vimana or Deula, is the sanctum enshrining the deity the porch or assembly hall called

Jagamohana is the place for the congregation of devotees. The former, constructed on a square base, has a soaring curvilinear tower (sikhara) and is known as rekha deula. The laatter built on a rectangular base is a pidha temple, i.e. its roof consists of pidhas which are horizontal platforms arranged successively iii a receding formation so as to constitute a pyramidal superstructure.- Although the two temples are architecturally different, they are constructed in axial alignment and interconnected so as to form an integral pattern.

This two-part structure in the earliest form of temple construction is noticeable in the Parsurameswar temple of Bhubaneswar (7th century). A modest specimen of the Bhubaneswar-Lakshmaneswar group of early temples, it has a squattish type of curvilinear sikhara and an oblong pillared jagamohana.

The scupltures on the temple walls are also notable for their simplicity and beauty. The Kalinga style reached its perfection during the Ganea period when two more structures were added the front of the two-part temple in order to meet the needs of the elaborate rituals; these are the natamandira (dancing hall) and the bhogamandapa (hall of offerings). The four halls of structure as at Lingaraja and Jagannatha, stand in one line with emphasis on the towering sikhara of the main shrine. However, the devotees have to enter through the side doors of the jagamohana leaving the tamandira and bhogamandapa behind.

Temple building activities in Odisha continued uninterrupted between the 7th and 16th centuries.

As different religious sects had their successive sway over the land during this period, they provided the necessary fillip for modifications in the architectural designs and sculptural details.

The Vaital temple at Bhubaneswar and the Varahi temple at Chaurasi in the Prachi Valley with their semicylindrical roofs are examples of a different order of temples described as E(hakhara type in the shiIpasastras. The former with its tower resembling a topsy-turvied boat and the later with its barrel-vaulted top are dedicated to the goddess Chamunda and Varahi respectively. The silhouetted interior of the sanctum and the sculptural motifs in the niches of the temples bear the influence of Shakti cult.

There is yet another class of temples which are almost unique in their conception and execution in the whole country; these are the circular shaped, hypaethral or roofless structures dedicated to the sixty-four yoginis belonging to the Tantric order. Out of all the five shrines of yogini worship existing in the whole country, two are situated in Odisha, the Chausathi Yogini temples one at Hirapur near Bhubancswar and the other at Ranipur-Jharial in Titlagarh subdivision of Balangir district. At the center of these temples is pedestalled the image of Bhairava around which are located the yoginis, each in a niche. The artistic figures of the yoginis, their hair style varying totally in case of each at Hirapur, are superb in execution.

However, the Kalinga style of architecture which was the most common order throughout progressed well under the patronage of the Somavamsi Kings of Odisha during the 10th and 11th centuries.

The Mukteswar temple(10th century) of Bhubaneswar is considered a "gem of Odisha architecture"and is accepted as one of the most beautiful temples of India. Elegantly decorated from top to bottom, it stands within a gracefully laid out compound with an exquisite makara torana in front. The rekha sikhara and rhythmic in treatment, is unrivalled in beauty. The Jagmohana is a harmonious pidha deula crowned with a kalasa at the top. The Rajarani temple (11th century) owing its name to a type of stone known as 'rajarania' is an architectural specimen of the later Somavamsi period. Picturesquely set amidst a wide expanse of rice fields, this temple in its execution combines grace and elegance, beauty of form and sculptural embellishments The deula, adorned with a cluster of miniature temples is reminiscent of Khajuraho. The Brahmeswar temple (11th century) characteristic continuation of the Drissan style.

The great temple of Lingaraja (11th century) at Bhubaneswar is the quintessence of Odisha architecture With all the features of temple architecture fully developed and perfectly executed, it is undoubted one of the most finished temples in India. The eladorate temple complex consisting of the lowering sikhara (45 m. in height), jagamohana, natamandira and bhogamandap all in perfact harmony along with the lesser shrines around has a unique grander and majesty. There are a very large number of temples of different order in Bhbaneswar which may be called a veritable museum of temples.

The temple of Jagannatha at Puri is the earliest Ganga monument of Odisha .The massive edifice standing on a high platform connected with the ground led by a flight of 22 steps is the product of accumulated experience of the past temple architecture. The whole of the main temple was covered by a thick consisting of plaster, which earned for it the name 'White Pagoda'. The plaster has since been removed by the Archaeological Survey of India to reveal the beautiful stone carvings.

FESTIVALS IN ODISHA (ORISSA)

Fairs & Festivals in Odisha (Orissa) - With numerous religions, ancient temples, local shrines, tribes and an array of sacred places, Odisha (Orissa) observes uncountable number of festivals and fairs round the year. Major Odisha(Orissa) Festivals of Odisha is Jagannath Puri Rath Yatra and Durga Pooja. Three different religions flourished on the holy land of Odisha (Orissa) thus making it mandatory to celebrate various religious Odisha festivals with great fanfare. Odisha Cultural & Religious Festivals are very famous in india.

A land of varied cultures and traditions, Odisha (Orissa) automatically serves to be a land of festivals. Religion or folklores, tradition or agriculture and seasonal variations or ethnic dance forms; all serve to be a setting for the celebration. Odisha (Orissa) celebrates one or other festival every month giving an opportunity to the visitors and natives both to enjoy and have real fun. With some of the special rituals attached to each, these festivals add bright colors to the landscape of Odisha (Orissa)'s cultural heritage. Some of the festivals of this land of Lord Jagannath are dedicated to His holy self. Some other festivals celebrated in Odisha (Orissa) find a close resemblance to a lot of festivals of North India; however they are called by different names and are even celebrated in a different fashion. But amazingly, every festivity centers around the prayer sacraments to seek the blessings of gods, exchanging goodwill, distributing sweets, decorating houses, wearing new clothes, music, dance and feasting. Whatever is the way, each festival really makes the country come alive throughout the year.

Durga Puja and Kali Puja are the two major festivals of the land that showcase the power of the Shakti worship cult in Odisha (Orissa). Celebrated with utmost earnestness, joviality and eclat, this festival celebrated in the months of September and October truly offer an opportunity for a larger than life type celebration. Other festivals like Rath Yatra of Lord Jagannath, Dola Purnima, Konark Dance Festival and Puri Beach Festival accompanied by some tribal festivals are also celebrated with much gusto here.

Out of all the festivals celebrated in Odisha (Orissa), Rath Yatra - a grand procession carried out in the honor of the presiding deity of Puri is celebrated in the most pompous way possible.

FAIRS AND FESTIVALS IN ORISSA (ODISHA)

Travel to Orissa, a fascinating land that mesmerizes its visitors like no other. From ancient temples to delightful beaches, this state is indeed a wonderful destination to travel to. Making it all the more appealing are the varied fairs and festivals in Orissa that are a fine extension of the state's identity and culture.

The fairs and festivals in Orissa are characterized by a rich presence of color interspersed with a gaiety that simply delights every onlooker. Some of the fairs and festivals in Orissa also display a deep religious fervor that touches all. Among the most famous events in Orissa are the Lord Jagannath Festivals that attract visitors from all across the world. The Konark Festival and the Puri Beach Festival also feature among the most important fairs and festivals in Orissa. Seasonal festivals or religious festivals, you can find them all as you check the fairs and festivals calendar of Orissa.

A travel to Orissa can add up to a very memorable experience. And if you spice that up with a visit to some of its delightful fairs and festivals, you surely have a most wonderful vacation on your platter.

10

Education

INTRODUCTION

Panoramic View of Ravenshaw University, Cuttack

Educational Institutions

1. Indian Institute of Technology (IIT) at Bhubaneswar
2. National Institute of Technology Rourkela (NIT) at Rourkela
3. Indian Institute of Management (IIM-SB) at Sambalpur
4. Indian Institutes of Science Education and Research (IISER) at Brahmapur
5. National Institute of Science Education and Research (NISER) at Bhubaneswar

6. All India Institute of Medical Sciences (AIIMS) at Bhubaneswar

7. Veer Surendra Sai University of Technology (VSSUT) at Burla

8. National Law University at Cuttack

9. International Institute of Information Technology (IIIT) at Bhubaneswar

10. Berhampur University at Brahmapur

11. Biju Patnaik University of Technology at Rourkela

12. Buxi Jagabandhu Bidyadhar College at Bhubaneswar

13. Central University of Orissa at Koraput

14. College of Agriculture, Bhawanipatna

15. College of Engineering and Technology at Bhubaneswar

16. Dharanidhar College at Keonjhar

17. Fakir Mohan University at Balasore

18. Gangadhar Meher University at Sambalpur

19. Government College of Engineering, Kalahandi at Bhawanipatna

20. Hi-Tech Medical College & Hospital, Bhubaneswar at Bhubaneswar

21. Indira Gandhi Institute of Technology at Sarang

22. KIIT University at Bhubaneswar

23. Khallikote University at Brahmapur

24. Maharaja Krishna Chandra Gajapati Medical College and Hospital at Brahmapur

25. National Institute of Science and Technology at Brahmapur

26. North Orissa University at Baripada

27. Odisha State Open University at Sambalpur

28. Orissa University of Agriculture and Technology at Bhubaneswar

29. Parala Maharaja Engineering College at Brahmapur

30. Rama Devi Women's University at Bhubaneswar

31. Ravenshaw University at Cuttack
32. Sambalpur University at Sambalpur
33. Shri Ramachandra Bhanj Medical College at Cuttack
34. Siksha O Anusandhan University at Bhubaneswar
35. Utkal University at Bhubaneswar
36. Utkal University of Culture at Bhubaneswar
37. Veer Surendra Sai Medical College at Burla
38. Xavier Institute of Management, Bhubaneswar
39. Xavier University, Bhubaneswar
40. Institute of Mathematics and Applications, Bhubaneswar
41. Sri Sri University at Cuttack
42. Centurion University at Jatni, Bhubaneswar
43. National Institute of Rehabilitation Training and Research at Cuttack
44. National Institute of Social Work and Social Science, Bhubaneswar (NISWASS)
45. Pandit Raghunath Murmu Medical College and Hospital, Baripada
46. Saheed Laxman Nayak Medical College and Hospital, Koraput

Entry to various institutes of higher education especially into engineering degrees is through a centralised Odisha Joint Entrance Examination, conducted by the Biju Patnaik University of Technology (BPUT), Rourkela, since 2003, where seats are provided according to order of merit. Few of the engineering institutes enroll students by through Joint Entrance Examination. For medical courses, there is a corresponding All India Pre Medical Test.

EDUCATION IN ODISHA

Previously a neglected aspect of the state, which was not a focus of the Indian Central government, Education in Odisha is witnessing a rapid transformation. Its capital city, Bhubaneswar, is emerging as a knowledge hub in India with several new public and private universities, including the establishment of an Indian Institute of Technology after five decades of demand.

Odisha has fared reasonably well in terms of literacy rates. The overall literacy rate according to Census 2011 is 73.5%, which is marginally behind of the national average of 74.04%. In Odisha there are also many schools and colleges, maintained by government.

History

Ancient and medieval era

Historically, Odisha has been at the forefront of education and research. The ruins of a major ancient university, Puspagiri, were recently discovered in Odisha. Scholars from far away lands, such as Greece, Persia and China used to study philosophy, astronomy, mathematics and science at this famed university. Along with Takshashila and Nalandauniversities, Puspagiri was among the oldest universities in the world. All three universities were mentioned by the Chinese traveler Huien Tsang (Xuanzang), who visited India in the 7th century, but unlike the others, the whereabouts of Puspagiri university were unknown until recently. As of 2007, the ruins of this university have not been fully excavated yet.Odisha's education prospered under Hindu and Buddhist rule. However, it went into a period of decline under the Sun dynasty, after 1568. The Muslims and the Marathas, who occupied Odisha before the British, did little to spread education. Before the creation of modern Odisha, the mainstay of the education system were the Sanskrit *Pathsalas*, and the *Maktabs*, which existed in Cuttack, Balasore, Puri, Angul and Sambalpur, local *Chatasalis* to cater to grassroot level education, as well as advanced centers of Oriental learning.

Colonial era

The colonialization of Odisha by the British East India Company in 1803 proved disastrous to Odisha in all spheres. It led to the collapse of the traditional education system. Yet,

Odisha being one of the last Indian territories to come under the British rule became exposed much later than other parts of India to the system of education they introduced. Under the East India Company, Christian missionaries who took up printing the Old and New Testaments in Odia, also contributed to some growth in education. The first primary school was created in 1822 by missionaries.

The Cuttack Zilla school, Odisha's first modern school up to matriculation level, was established in 1866. It was extended to become a Collegiate school in 1868, which provided first and second year college education to Odia students. However, Odias were severely disadvantaged by having to attend Presidency College in Kolkata for B.A. degrees. This was until the collegiate branch of Zilla school was converted into a full bachelor's degree granting college under the then commissioner, T. E. Ravenshaw. This college was named as Ravenshaw College after him.

Women's education was taken up with the establishment of the Ravenshaw Hindu Girls' School in 1873. The Maharajah of Keonjhar, the Rani or Talcher, amongst other notable Odia personalities, who made contributions. Later, Reba Ray, a former student of this school and Sailabala Das became instrumental in furthering the cause of women's education, leading to the creation of the Sailabala Women's College, Cuttack.

Medical education began with the opening of the first medical school in 1876, by Dr. Stewart, the Civil Surgeon of Cuttack, who also translated the *Materia Medica* into Odia. The first industrial school was opened in 1884, in Alalpur, Balasore. A survey school began at the same time in Cuttack, which later on became the Orissa School of Engineering, marking the beginnings of technical education in the state.

School education

Literacy

Although 10 years of primary education is mandatory in Odisha, the literacy rate is only 73.5%, which is marginally behind of the national average of 74.04%. The government of

India has undertaken steps to improve women's literacy in the tribal pockets in the state and elsewhere in India. Male literacy is 75.95% and female literacy is 50.97%.

Among the districts, Malkangiri has the lowest literacy rate of 31.26%. Among the women, lowest literacy level is in Nabarangpur district, at 21.02%, and Malkangiri district at 21.28%.Khurda district which includes Bhubaneswar city, has the highest literacy of 80.19%.

This district also has the highest female literacy of 71.06%. The high literacy figures of Khurda district is certainly influenced by the inclusion of the state capital in the statistics. Next to Khurda comes Jagatsinghpur district with 79.61% literates. The literacy level in Orissa at 63.61% is comparable with all-India average of 65.38%. However, there are considerable regional disparities between areas, and communities. Non-formal and adult literacy programs are run in various districts and are at different stages of implementation. Out of 30 districts, 9 are continuing total literacy campaign [TLC]. 10 districts are either continuing or awaiting approval of post literacy program [PLP]. 11 districts have completed PLP, and some of them have received sanction for Continuing Education Program. The State Government is committed to the Universalisation of Elementary Education in the State with the aim of fulfilling the constitutional obligation with the assistance of Central Government.

Odisha Adarsha Vidyalayas (OAVs)

One of the major innovation in recent years has been plans of Odisha State to setup one Odisha Adarsha Vidyalaya(OAV) (literally Odisha Model School) at each of 314 block headquarters. 100 Odisha Adarsha Vidyalayas(OAVs) has already started functioning from academic session 2016-17. These Adarsha Vidyalayas would be CBSE affiliated fully residential schools, provide free of education, and target talented students through an annual entrance examination. These would have Class VI through Class XII and each class would have 80 number of students.

Universalisation of elementary education

Keeping in view the need for Universalisation of elementary education, there has been expansion at Primary and Upper Primary School stage of education, in the Government sector, especially in rural areas as well as backward areas.

Status of elementary education in the state

In Odisha there are 35,928 Primary and 20,427 Upper Primary schools to provide education at elementary level. More 491 New Primary and 490 New Upper Primary schools opened under S.S.A. to provide schooling in unserved areas.

- 66 lakh children of 6–14 years age group are in-school, out of which 12 lakh are SC and 17 lakh are ST.
- 1.87 lakh children of 6–14 years age group are out-of-school from which 0.3 lakh are from SC and 0.9 lakh are from ST community. Out of them 56,995 Children were admitted to regular existing & New Schools under Enrolment Drive in districts.

Further to improve access to Elementary Education and to achieve 100% enrolment, Government have relaxed the norm for opening of new Primary schools

- In K.B.K. districts and Tribal Sub Plan areas new primary schools will be opened in habitations having at least 25 children in the 6–14 years age group provided there is no primary school within one KM of such habitations.
- In all the districts the distance norm for opening of new primary and new upper primary schools is relaxed in case of natural barrier like river, hilly terrain, dense forest etc.
- There are 218 Minority and Mission Managed Primary Schools, wherein 599 teachers are receiving grant-in-aid from the Government. Besides, Odia Medium Schools.
- Odisha_Adarsha_Vidyalaya Sangathan
- Gram Vikas Residential School was established in 1982 at Kankia village in Ganjam district. Mahendra Tanaya Ashram School was established in Koinpur village in

Gajapati District of Odisha in 1992. Two more schools, Gram Vikas Shiksa Niketan and Gram Vikas Vidya Vihar were established in 1998 and 2002 in Kalahandi district and Ganjam district respectively.

UNIVERSALISATION OF SECONDARY EDUCATION

Secondary Education

There are 6193 Govt. and aided Secondary Schools, 849 Recognized High Schools and 151 permitted High Schools in the State.

- As per the GIA Rules, 2004, 1981 private High Schools have been notified to receive block grant.
- 1375 nos. of Contract Teachers has been engaged against the 3210 posts advertised.
- Contract teachers of High Schools have been allowed the minimum basic pay of their respective regular scale in Revised Scale of Pay 2008.
- Government have approved 799 candidates as non-teaching staff under the Rehabilitation Assistance Scheme in the year 2010.
- Computer Literacy is being popularized in High Schools. Board of Secondary Education has included computer learning as an optional subject in the curriculum for Secondary schools.

Rastriya Madhyamik Shiksha Abhiyan (RMSA)

RMSA is a national flagship programme initiated in 2009-10 to universalise Secondary Education by making good quality education available, accessible and affordable to all children within the age group of 14 – 18 years with strong focus on the elements of gender, equity & justice.

Objectives

- To provide secondary school within 5 km and higher secondary school within 7–10 km of every habitation.

- Gross Enrolment Ratio (GER) of 75% for class-IX & X within five years (by 2013-14).
- Universal Access to Secondary Education (SE) by 2017.
- Universal Retention by 2020.
- Access to Secondary Education (SE) for all disadvantaged group of children.
- To improve quality of education resulting in enhanced intellectual, social and cultural learning.

Action Taken

- Annual Work Plan for 2010-11 and Perspective Plan for 5 years submitted to GOI.
- PAB approved for 2009–10 Rs.207.18 crores and for 2010-11 Rs. 507.92 crore.
- Rs. 3.00 crores released by GOI for "Preparatory Activities" such as Strengthening State and District offices.
- Strengthening manpower ganising training/workshop/SEMI Setc.
- Rs. 71.40 crores released by GOI for "Project Activities" such as; Civil works for new school.
- M.M.E.R. (Management Monitoring Evaluation & Research which is being released to all the 30 districts.
- Data collection, data entry and analysis of "Secondary Education Management Information System" (S.E.M.I.S.), 2009-10 is completed & is under verification by the Inspector of Schools.

The 10+2 structure

In Odisha, as elsewhere in India, children are enrolled in school at the age of five. The core subjects taught in schools include Science (including Physics, Chemistry and Biology), Mathematics (Arithmetic, Algebra, Geometry, Trigonometry, Computer Science, and Set theory), Social Studies (Geography, History, Civics and Economics), and three languages, which are usually Odia, Hindi and English. Additionally, school children receive training in sports and physical education, as well as vocational training.

After ten years of schooling, children at the end of class(X) must appear in one of the three school examinations; 1. All India Secondary School Examination (AISSE), which is conducted by the Central Government run Central Board of Secondary Education (CBSE), 2. Odisha High School Certificate Examination, which is conducted by the Board of Secondary Education, Odisha(BSE) and 3. Indian Certificate of Secondary Education (ICSE) examination, conducted annually by the New Delhi-based Council for the Indian School Certificate Examinations (CISCE).

Children who appear in either the All India Secondary School Examination or the Odisha High School Certificate Examination have a choice of using Odia or Hindi or English as the medium language. However, the Council for the Indian School Certificate Examinations makes English the mandatory language.

Two years of higher secondary education follow, which is optional. Students, usually in the 15 through 17 age group, have a choice of specializing in the following streams;

1. Arts
2. Science
3. Commerce

At this stage, the students get exposed to a wide array of elective subjects. The CBSE conducts the All India Senior School Certificate Examination and the CISCE conducts the Indian School Certificate Examinations for students in class XII. There are also Junior colleges and Degree colleges in the state that offer secondary education for class XII children. The Council of Higher Secondary Education, Odisha (CHSE) conducts the higher secondary level examination for them.

This educational structure in Odisha is referred to commonly as the 10+2 system. Students who undergo the 10+2 education system are eligible for admission into a college or university in Odisha, and can also opt for other professional training.

However, admission into the few top institutions in Odisha, particularly in engineering and medicine, are highly competitive. Students graduating from class XII typically must qualify in an entrance examination in order to gain admission.

Odisha Joint Entrance Examination

The Government of Odisha conducts a highly competitive Joint Entrance Examination (OJEE) annually to select students for admission into the various engineering colleges operating under BPUT. In the year 2010, around 73,587 students appeared the OJEE against 76,000 students last year. Out of them 51,174 students sat for engineering, 19,663 , in MBA, 9,446 ,in MCA.

NATIONAL LEVEL PUBLIC INSTITUTIONS

Odisha has become a hub for higher education and has numerous inistitutions which are nationally and internationally recognised.

Biju Patnaik National Steel Institute

Biju Patnaik National Steel Institute (BPNSI), Puri is an autonomous Institute constituted by Ministry of Steel, Government of India was established on 1 January 2002 for the development of steel sector with an emphasis on the secondary steel sector. BPNSI is one of the few institutes in the country and the only institute in Odisha that offers a curriculum in Iron & Steel manufacturing & Plant Management. Currently the Institute is offering a one and half year "Advanced Certificate Course on Iron and Steel Manufacturing & Plant Management." The Institute plans to offer Degree and P.G. Diploma courses in the future.

Central Institute of Plastics Engineering and Technology

Central Institute of Plastic Engineering and Technology, Bhubaneswar established in 1986 is one of the 15 state-of-the-art centers spread across India devoted to academic, technology support & research (ATR) activities for the growth of plastics

& allied industries in the country. CIPET, Bhubaneswar has a track record of best performance centre consistently for last few years and rated to be the best centre. The institute offers B.Tech, M.Tech and PhD program on Plastics Engineering and Technology in affiliation with Biju Patnaik University of Technology.

Central Rice Research Institute

The Central Rice Research Institute (CRRI) is located in the city of Cuttack. It is one of the premier institutions in Asia for rice research. It was established by the center in 1946 with an experimental farm land of 0.6 km^2 provided by the Odisha government. It is the second largest institution dedicated to rice research after the one at Manila. The Institute has two research stations- Central Rainfed Upland Rice Research Station (CRURRS), Hazaribagh, in Jharkhand, and the Regional Rainfed Lowland Rice Research Station (RRLRRS), Gerua, in Assam. These research stations were established to tackle the problems of rainfed uplands, and flood prone rainfed lowlands, respectively. Two Krishi Vigyan Kendras (KVKs) also function under the CRRI located at Santhapur, Cuttack and Jainagar, Koderma.

Central Tool Room & Training Centre

Central Tool Room & Training Centre, Bhubaneswar is an autonomous institute under the Ministry of MSME, Government of India. Since 1991 imparting industry oriented long & short term training programmes on CAD/CAM, Tool Design & Manufacturing, Tool & Die Making, Diploma in Mechatronics, CNC Programming & Machining, Machine Maintenance, CCNA, Industrial Automation, VLSI, Hardware & Networking Management, ITI (Machinist/Welder) etc.

Central University of Orissa

The Central University of Orissa has been established in Koraput by the Parliament under the Central Universities Act, 2009 (No. 3C of 2009). It is one of the 15 new Central Universities established by the Government of India during the UGC XI Plan period to address the concerns of "equity and access" and as per the policy of the Government of India to increase the access to quality higher education by people in less educationally developed districts which have a Graduate Enrollment Ratio of less than the national average of 11%.

Institute of Dental Sciences

Institute of Dental Sciences, Bhubaneswar was set up in 2005 on the recommendation of Dental Council of India, Health and Family Welfare Department, Govt. of India. It has been conducting B.D.S Course from the academic session 2006-07.

Indian Institute of Handloom Technology

I.I.H.T. Bargarh, the fifth central sector institute came into existence on June 2, 2008. Initially it started functioning in the panchayat college campus in Bargarh township which is a prominent place in western part of Odisha. The permanent campus is under construction on Bargarh-Bhatli road, 8 km from the district headquarters. It offers a diploma course in handloom and textile technology.

Institute of Life Sciences

The Institute of Life Sciences (ILS), an autonomous institute has been brought under the fold of the Department of Biotechnology, Government of India in August 2002. The institute is located in close proximity to other research institutions at Bhubaneswar. The institute was earlier established on February 11, 1989 and was under the administrative and financial control of Department of Science and Technology, Government of Odisha. Prime minister of India, Atal Bihari Vajpayee dedicated the institute to the nation on July 15, 2003 with a declaration to develop the institute as a "National Centre for Excellence". The mandate of ILS is to undertake basic and translational research in frontier areas of life sciences. The research interests of the faculty are in three major areas: (a) Infectious Disease Biology, (b) Gene Function and Regulation and (c) Translation Research and Technology

Development. In addition, new collaborations with industry have been established to tap commercial potential of laboratory science.

Indian Institute of Mass Communication

IIMC Dhenkanal, was set up in August 1993 as the first branch of IIMC New Delhi, under the Ministry of Information and Broadcasting, Govt. of India. It imparts education and training in journalism and also undertakes media studies and research. The Institute conducts PG Diploma courses in Journalism in English and Odia, besides short term courses and workshops.

Institute of Physics

The Institute Of Physics, Bhubaneswar is an autonomous research institution funded jointly by the Department Of Atomic Energy (DAE) and the Government of Odisha. It provides research facilities for postgraduate research.

Indian Institute of Public Health

Indian Institute of Public Health, Bhubaneswar is one of the four institutes set up by PHFI as a part of its charter to build public health capacity in India. IIPH, Bhubaneswar, commenced its academic activities from August 2010. The institute offers a Post Graduate Diploma course in Public Health Management, launched on 2 August 2010. Government doctors from Odisha and Chhattisgarh and self-sponsored candidates are participating in this course. In addition to this, various short term training programmes, workshops and research activities are being undertaken by the institute.

Indian Institute of Technology

The Indian Institute of Technology, Bhubaneswar is the third and one of the largest of eight new Indian Institutes of Technology established by the MHRD, Government of India in 2008–2009. A total of 935 acres (3.78 km) of land has been allocated at Arugul towards the self-contained campus for 10,000 students and 1,100 faculty, making it the second largest of all IITs after the one at Kharagpur, and largest IIT in any metropolitan location.

As of 2009, there are undergraduate programs leading to B. Tech degrees in civil engineering, electrical engineering, and mechanical engineering. Postgraduate students are being admitted into the M. Tech and PhD programs.

Indian Institute of Management

The Indian Institute of Management, Sambalpur is the 14th Indian Institute of Management established by the MHRD, Government of India in 2015. A total of 237 acres (0.96 km) of land has been allocated at Basantpur towards the state of art permanent campus

The institute has started Post Graduation Program (PGP) in Management since 2015.

International Institute of Information Technology

International Institute of Information Technology, Bhubaneswar is an information technology higher education institute established in 2006 by the Government of Odisha. It has been converted to an unitary university on January 20, 2014. It offers Masters and Bachelors programme in Engineering. It is considered as an institute of national importance according to the AICTE.

Indian Institute of Tourism and Travel Management

Indian Institute of Tourism and Travel Management (IITTM), Bhubaneswar is one of the five premier autonomous institutes set by Ministry of Tourism, Government of India. IITTM is engaged in teaching, training, research and consultancy and is the only institute in the country dedicated to the tourism learning. The institute at Bhubaneswar was in 1996 as Baji Rout Regional Center for Eastern India with the primary objective of expanding its activities to a part of the country that is full of tourism potential. It offers two years postgraduate diploma in management specializing in Tourism and Travel and International Business.

Institute of Minerals and Materials Technology

The Institute of Minerals and Materials Technology IMMT, (formerly Regional Research Laboratory, Bhubaneswar) was set up as a premier establishment of the Council of Scientific & Industrial Research (CSIR), New Delhi in 1964 in the State of Odisha, in eastern India. The laboratory specializes in providing R&D support for process and product development with special emphasis on conservation and sustainable utilization of natural resources. Over the years, IMMT has developed S&T capabilities in a wide range of areas from mineralogy to materials engineering. The laboratory has expertise in conducting technology oriented programmes in mining and mineral/bio-mineral processing, metal extraction and materials characterization, process engineering, industrial waste management, pollution monitoring and control, marine and forest products development, utilization of medicinal and aromatic plants and appropriate technologies for societal development.

National Institute of Fashion Technology

National Institute of Fashion Technology(NIFT), Bhubaneswar center is one of the latest additions to the existing countrywide gamut of NIFT. It started functioning from June 2010 from its transit campus situated in Centurion Institute of Technology, near HP Gas Plant, Bhubaneswar. The course being offered at the institute at present, include specialization in two disciplines, Bachelor of Design in Textile Design and Master of Fashion Management Studies. The institute boasts of eminent and experienced faculty to facilitate quality education from the very commencement of the center. A total of 35 acres (140,000 m^2) of land have been granted by the state government. The NIFT would be funded through the Indian Ministry of Commerce. It is admitting students from 2010.

National Institute of Rehabilitation Training and Research

The National Institute of Rehabilitation Training and Research (NIRTAR) is an autonomous body established in 1975 under the Ministry of Social Justice and Empowerment, Govt. of India. It is located in a beautiful rural area at Olatpur, 30 km from Cuttack and Bhubaneswar. It conducts three bachelor's degree courses in Physiotherapy, Occupational Therapy, Prosthetics and Orthotics, two Postgraduate courses in Occupational Therapy and Physiotherapy affiliated to Utkal University, Bhubaneswar.

It also has an accreditation for DNB in Physical Medicine and Rehabilitation of National Board of Examination (NBE), New Delhi.

National Institute of Science Education & Research

The National Institute of Science Education and Research (NISER) is a premier research institution in India along the lines of the internationally reputed IISc in Bangalore, and five sister institutions, the IISERs. Instead of the Ministry of Human Resources Development, NISER operates under the umbrella of the Department of Atomic Energy (DAE). It was established in 2007, in Bhubaneswar, Odisha, when the first batch of students were admitted into its integrated postgraduate programs.

NISER is dedicated to graduate education and research only. It offers M.S.,5 year integrated M.S. as well as PhD degrees in physics, chemistry, mathematics, and biology. The Odisha government has provided 301 acres (1.2 km^2)of land free of cost for the upcoming campus at Jatani near Bhubaneswar.

Keeping in view the paucity of central government institutions in the state, the Government of Odisha has mooted the idea of a National Institute for Technology Education and Research (NITER), a sister institution of NISER, in Bhubaneswar.

National Institute of Technology

Established in the year 1961, The National Institute of Technology (NIT) located at the steel city of Rourkela is the foremost engineering degree granting institutions in Odisha. It has consistently been ranked among the top engineering institutes in the country, most recently being placed as the 3rd best Engineering Institute in Eastern India, after IIT Kharagpurand IIT Guwahati by DataQuest.

National Law University of Orissa

A national law university was established in 2009 at Naraj, in the outskirts of the city of Cuttack. The university offers integrated B.A. LL.B. and B.B.A. LL.B., integrated LL.M-PH.D and Ph.D. courses.

National University

A national university for research is being set up in Bhubaneswar. The government of India will seek expertize from leading universities, such as Yale, MIT and Princeton, in setting up the national university at Bhubaneswar.

All India Institute of Medical Sciences, Bhubaneswar

All India Institute of Medical Sciences, Bhubaneswar (AIIMS) is being set up in the state under the Pradhan Mantri Swasthya Suraksha Yojna. Former Prime Minister Atal Bihari Vajpayee had laid the foundation stone for the super-speciality hospital in 2003. The state AIIMS was then estimated to cost about Rs 820.49 crore. The institute has initiated the process of recruiting staff and is buying equipment simultaneously and the facility would be ready to take admissions in undergraduate medical courses by 2013. Work on the medical college and the hospital buildings would be complete by September 2012. The Union government recently selected three top medical institutes to mentor the six upcoming AIIMS prototypes. AIIMS New Delhi will mentor its clone in Bhubaneswar. The mentor will guide the upcoming institute in selecting faculty and setting up necessary infrastructure.

Rashtriya Sanskrit Sansthan (Deemed University), Shri Sadashiva Campus

This campus was established on 1971 and is situated at Puri in Odisha. The institution is more than 100 years old.

The campus is pursuing research work leading to the degree of Vidyavaridhi (PhD) and imparting education in Sahitya, Dharma Shastra, Navya Vyakarana, Puranetihas, Jyotish, Advaita Vedanta, Navya Nyaya, Sarvadarshana and Sankhya Yoga at post–graduate and graduate level and Shiksha Shastri at graduate level.

Regional Institute of Education

A premier centre of education research, the Regional Institute of Education is located near Acharya Vihar in Bhubaneswar. It is a regional centre of NCERT serving the eastern region. Apart from running training programmes for teachers of schools and colleges, the institute also has integrated courses of B.Sc and B.Ed. The institute also runs courses on B.Ed., M.Ed. and M.Phil (Education).

Regional Medical Research Centre

Regional Medical Research Centre(RMRC), Bhubaneswar, was established in 1981 by Indian Council of Medical Research. It conducts interdisciplinary research on locally prevailing communicable and non-communicable diseases. It provides training and research to post graduate students for Ph.D./ MD degree, MSc. dissertation and short term training to the doctors and technicians from state health departments and NVBDCP, Delhi.

State level public institutions

Berhampur University

Berhampur University was established in southern Odisha in 1965, as the third oldest university in the state. The university has 25 affiliated colleges and covers the districts of Gajapati,

Ganjam, Kandhamal, Koraput, Malkangiri, Nabarangpur and Rayagada.

Biju Patnaik University of Technology

The Biju Patnaik University of Technology (BPUT), Rourkela, was created by an act of the Odisha state legislature in the year 2002. Almost all the engineering, pharmacy, architecture and most of the colleges offering MBA degree programmes are either constituent or affiliated colleges of BPUT. Today, the university has 110 colleges, both constituent and affiliated, with around 58,000 students. The disciplines include engineering and architecture, business management and hotel management, computer studies and pharmacy.

College of Engineering and Technology

The College of Engineering and Technology (CET-B) was initially established within the preview of OUAT in Bhubaneswar. It got separated from OUAT since 2002, having its own vast campus of about 139 acres (0.56 km) in Ghatikia, Khandagiri. It is a primarily an undergraduate college, offering programs in Architecture, Computer science, Information Technology, Electrical, Civil, Instrumentation & Electronics, Bio-Technology, Mechanical engineering, Textile engineering and Fashion Technology. It is currently affiliated to BPUT (Biju Patnaik University of Technology). It places about 75% of its students every year and has a large number of students interning all over India .

Government College Of Engineering, Keonjhar

Government College of Engineering, Keonjhar is the only Government engineering college in North Odisha. The institute started under the Department of Industries, Government of Odisha in 1956 offering Diploma education in Mining Engineering and later in 1995 introduced degree curriculum. Electrical Engineering and Mechanical Engineering branches were added in 1997. In 2006, the government of Odisha declared Orissa School of Mining Engineering (Degree Stream) as a constitute college of Biju Pattnaik University of Technology, Rourkela under self finance mode to develop it as a centre of excellence in the field of Engineering & Technology. In 2008, Mineral Engineering and in 2009, Metallurgical & Materials Engineering were added. In 2011, as per a government notification, it has been declared as a full-fledged government engineering college. In 2015, Computer Science & Engineeringand Civil Engineering were added.

Fakir Mohan University

Fakir Mohan University, Vyasa Vihar, Balasore was established by the Government of Odisha, in 1999.

Indira Gandhi Institute of Technology

The Indira Gandhi Institute of Technology (IGIT) is located at Sarang in the industrial belt of Talcher. It was established in 1982 by the government of Odisha. In addition to four year undergraduate degrees in electrical, mechanical, chemical and civil engineering, and metallurgical & materials science, it offers three year diplomas in a few technical disciplines.

Institute of Mathematics and Applications

The Institute of Mathematics and Applications, (IMA) located in Bhubaneswar is an academic institution, established by the government of Odisha to conduct advanced research in pure and applied mathematics, and to conduct advanced postgraduate degree programs in the field. It was established in 1999.

Maharaja Krishna Chandra Gajapati Medical College

The Maharaja Krishna Chandra Gajapati (MKCG) Medical College is a medical college in Berhampur. It was originally started in 1976 as an extension of the SCB Medical College. It operates under Berhampur University. It offers MBBS and MD degrees and also provides training in medical related fields.

North Orissa University

North Orissa University, Baripada is a public and open

university established in 1998. The jurisdiction of the University extends over two districts, Mayurbhanj and Keonjhar. There are 80 affiliated colleges, both general and professional, catering to the demand of higher education.

Orissa University of Agriculture and Technology

The Orissa University of Agriculture and Technology (OUAT) was established in the city of Bhubaneswar in 1962. It is dedicated to agriculture related research and education, and has seven colleges as well as a centre for postgraduate studies.

Parala maharaja engineering college(PMEC), Berhampur

PMEC Berhampur was estd:2009 by Govt. of Odisha, started functioning in its academic building at sitalapalli, berhampur with four branches. This college is a constituent college of BPUT, Odisha. College was inaugurated by Sri Naveen Patnaik, Hon'bl CM, Odisha.

Ravenshaw University

Ravenshaw Convention Centre, Ravenshaw University, Cuttack, Odisha

Upgraded from Ravenshaw College one of the oldest and largest colleges of India, the Ravenshaw University came into existence on 15 November 2006.

Originally affiliated to University of Calcutta and thereafter to Patna University and then finally to Utkal University the institution finally got its own identity and became one of the most reputed universities of the Odisha state.

Presently the university runs 23 Post-Graduate courses with research facilities and 27 Undergraduate honours courses.

Sambalpur University

Sambalpur University (Jyoti Vihar) in Burla, in western Odisha is another important university covering the districts of Bargarh, Bolangir, Boudh, Deogarh, Jharsugda, Kalahandi, Nuapada, Sambalpur, Subarnapur, Sundargarh as well as the Athamallik Sub-Division of Angul district.

It offers postgraduate education in twenty seven subjects. The university has been functioning since 1967.

Shriram Chandra Bhanja Medical College

Established in 1944, The Shriram Chandra Bhanja Medical College (SCB Medical College) at Cuttack, is the premier medical institution in Odisha and one of the oldest in India. It offers postgraduate degrees in all broad areas of medicine.

It also runs super speciality training facilities in several areas such as cardiology, neurosurgery, and radiotherapy. There also exists a dental wing under the SCB Medical college.

Shri Jagannath Sanskrit Vishvavidayalaya

Shri Jagannath Sanskrit Vishvavidayalaya was established in Puri by the erstwhile Chief Minister of Odisha Janaki Ballabh Pattanayak, an eminent scholar of Sanskrit, on 7 July 1981.

It is the third Sanskrit university of the country next to Sampurnananda Sanskrit University of Banaras and Kameswar Singh Sanskrit University of Darabhanga .

Utkal University

Utkal University (Vani Vihar) was the first university to be established in Odisha in 1943. It is also the seventeenth oldest in India. It is located in Bhubaneswar and has about 3,000 postgraduate and doctoral students enrolled. The university has jurisdiction over nine districts in Odisha, namely Angul, Cuttack, Dhenkanal, Jajpur, Jagatsinghpur, Kendrapara, Khurda, Nayagarh and Puri catering to the needs of higher education of a population of over 11 million people.

Main entrance to Utkal University

Utkal University of Culture

The Utkal University of Culture is a newly established institution located in Bhubaneswar.

Veer Surendra Sai Medical College

The Veer Surendra Sai (VSS) Medical college and hospital has been in operation since 1959 in Burla. It offers undergraduate and postgraduate education in medicine and surgery, besides offering training courses in pharmacy and nursing.

Veer Surendra Sai University of Technology, Burla

Established in 1956 at Burla, the Veer Surendra Sai University of Technology, Burla, formerly known as University College of Engineering (UCE) is Odisha's oldest, and one of the oldest and prestigious engineering institutions of East India.

Initially an autonomous college since 1991, it was elevated as a university in the year 2009, as a result of a move by the Government of Odisha to accord it with the status of a unitary university.

It offers undergraduate, postgraduate and doctoral degrees in several engineering disciplines. VSSUT receives financial grants from All India Council of Technical Education and University Grants Commission (India), two central government agencies, as well as from the state government.

While other major engineering institutions (such as the IITs) only enjoy deemed university status, VSSUT is one of India's full scale university for engineering and technology.

The campus covers an area of 203 acres (0.82 km2) with an expansion capacity up to 503 acres (2.04 km2), as per the land allotted to it. There is a proposal to upgrade this to NIT. In the year 2012 VSSUT was awarded 12B status by University Grants Commission (India).

PRIVATE INSTITUTIONS

Xavier Institute of Management, Bhubaneswar

The Xavier Institute of Management, Bhubaneswar (XIMB) was established in 1987.

It owes its origin to a contract between the government of Odisha and the Odisha Jesuit Society. XIMB is governed by a board consisting of representatives from the Odisha Jesuit Society, the government of India, the government of Odisha, and invited industrialists and academics.

XIMB has been ranked among the top 10 business schools in India. The institution offers postgraduate programs, leading to Masters and PhD degrees in business management, rural management, human resource management, sustainability management as well several professional training programs. It has a few research centers in areas such as entrepreneurship, utility regulation, small and micro enterprise development, and healthcare management. XIMB grown up to become "Xavier University". Now XIMB is an autonomous business school under Xavier University.

Xavier Institute of Management, Bhubaneswar is a premier business school in India

Siksha 'O' Anusandhan (SOA) Deemed to be University

Siksha 'O' Anusandhan gained Deemed to be University status from the UGC in 2007. SOA has the highest grade of 'A' from NAAC. Additionally, SUM Hospital (its affiliated hospital) has been awarded with the prestigious NABH accreditation.Link to SOA University's Website

Centurion University

Centurion University, Bhubaneswar is Odisha's first private state university.

Kalinga Institute of Industrial Technology Deemed to be University

A building of KIIT's School of Technology

The Kalinga Institute of Industrial Technology (KIIT) is established in Bhubaneswar in 1992. Academic programmes of KIIT University are conducted by its seven constituent schools – School of Technology, School of Computer Application, School of Management, School of Rural Management, School of Medicine, School of Biotechnology and KIIT Law School.

ICFAI University

Hyderabad based Institute of Chartered Financial Analysts of India (ICFAI) has signed a memorandum of understanding with the chief minister of Odisha, Mr. Naveen Patnaik, to set up a university in the outskirts of the city of Bhubaneswar. ICFAI plan to buy 150 acres (0.6 km) of land from private parties in Jatni, near the Khurda Road station. The university is budgeted at Rs. 150 crores (1.5 billion). It will function primarily as a business school.

Sri Sri University

Sri Sri University has been established under the Sri Sri University Act, 2009. The Government of Odisha has leased out about 187 acres of land near Bidyadharpur, Cuttack for the purpose of setting up the university. The total area of construction is expected to be 3,000,000 square feet and is slated to be completed in a phased manner in the next six years. On completion, the university campus will cater to the needs of 10000 students and around 2000 faculty staff. The university currently offers MBA programs in Agribusiness, General Management and Entrepreneurship.

Institutions through public-private partnership

Indian Institute of Information Technology, Brahmapur

In June 2007, the UPA government in New Delhi decided to establish a central government funded IIITs in each state. The IIIT in Odisha would be established in Brahmapur, and unlike its sister institute in Bhubaneswar, would receive funding from the center.

The IIIT at Berhampur is being established on a 100-acre (0.40 km^2) land and this is likely to be functional by end of 2009. This will help attracting more IT companies to South Odisha and the presence of STPI Brahmapur and IT Park at Brahmapur will also help. The Marine Bio-Technology Park is also planned for Brahmapur.

Sambalpur University Institute of Information Technology, Sambalpur

Thanks to Prof. Arun Pujari, Sambalpur university will get an Indian Institutes of Information Technology like IT institution.

Plans

Bhubaneswar as an emerging education hub

National institutes of excellence have been established recently in Bhubaneswar, while several more are planned, such as AIIMS, NISER, IIT, IIIT, and a National university. There are several prominent private universities, such as XIMB and ICFAI University. Other major upcoming prominent institutions, such as Sri Sri University, the National Law University of Orissa, as well as the world's biggest academic institution, Vedanta University, will be located in the neighboring cities of Cuttack and Puri. Institutions dedicated to research such as the Institute of Physics, and the Institute of Mathematics and Applications are also located here. The presence of so many quality institutions within close proximity of one another, is expected to stimulate academic excellence in and around Bhubaneswar, and serve as a catalyst for future growth. Additionally, the city also houses several Odisha government funded public universities, and over 70 technical institutions, which well above than any other city in eastern India. The city is also being promoted as an Information Technology Investment Region (ITIR) by the government. A total of 40 km^2 of land has been allocated for the purpose, out of which about 60% will be devoted to research and development. The Chief Minister of the state has asserted that Bhubaneswar is poised to emerge as India's foremost education hub.

Odisha Higher Education Vision 2020

The *Orissa Higher Education Vision 2020*, an effort organized by leading national and international researchers, scientists, and academicians of Odia origin, envisages a globally competitive higher education system in Orissa by 2020, with four tiered knowledge centers being developed throughout the state. An international level knowledge hub comparable to the San Francisco Bay Area or Boston metropolitan area in the USA is suggested in the rapidly expanding Bhubaneswar-Cuttack-Khurda-Puri metropolitan region. This will consist of several world class universities, technical and medical institutions, and laboratories, including NISER, IIT, IIIT, National University, National Law University, AIIMS, Vedanta University, Sri Sri University, NIPER, and several other new institutions to be established by the central government or through public-private partnership, as well as private institutions. At the second tier would be five other metropolitan regions, Rourkela, Sambalpur-Jharsuguda (IIHT Bargarh, OUAT branch at Chiplima, XIMB campus at Sambalpur, CIFT Burla, plan to upgrade VSS medical college and GM college to university status), Berhampur, Balasore-Baripada, and Jeypore-Koraput-Sunabeda, each with two universities, multiple engineering and medical colleges, as well as one or more national level institutions. The third tier knowledge hubs, located in all urban areas throughout the state, would have a university, an autonomous college, as well as a medical and an engineering college. Lastly, the fourth tier would include smaller towns, which would have at least an autonomous college and a trade school.

Under construction and planned medical and engineering colleges

Medical college Bhawanipatna Medical college Keonjhar by ahayog Healthcare and Research Foundation Medical college Jagatpur, Cuttack by ahayog Healthcare and Research Foundation Medical college Talcher by MCL Hitech medical college Rourkela Medical college Rourkela by SAIL upgrading the IGH Govt Medical college Bolangir and Balesore Central university Koraput will establish a medical college at Koraput ESIC medical college Bhubaneswar AIIMS Bhubaneswar Medical college at Angul. University in western Orissa with the partnership between govt and industries Upgradation

Jharsuguda engineering school to engineering college A medical college between jharsuguda and Sundargarh by the mines operating there A power management institute to be established at Jharsuguda 2 branch of XIMB bhubaneswar at Sambalpur and Bolangir

State legislation pertaining to higher education

The Odisha state legislative assembly (Vidhan Sabha) will be formulating a Private Universities Act to facilitate the growth of private universities such as Vedanta university, Sri Sri university. The higher education department of the state will draft the bill, which will be referred to the law department, before being placed in the assembly. This bill would guarantee the fiscal and administrative autonomy for private institutions.

Vedanta University act

The Odisha legislature was going to consider a specific act to make Vedanta university a statutory body. After the passage of the act, the university would have established its own, independent governing board, where the Odisha government would not exercise any control. Later news reports suggested that the plan for the Vedanta University was a "closed chapter"

Bibliography

Baird, Robert: *Religion in Modern India*, New Delhi, Manohar, 1981.

Beaumont, Roger : *Sword of the Raj: The British Army in India, 1747-1947*, Indianapolis, Bobbs-Merrill, 1977.

Brown, Judith M.: *Gandhi and Civil Disobedience*, London, Cambridge University Press, 1977.

Chase, Kenneth: *Firearms: A Global History to 1700*. Cambridge University Press, 2003.

Chaudhary, M.: *Partition and the Curse of Rehabilitation*, Calcutta, Bengal Rehabilitation Organization, 1964.

Cowan, Ruth Schwartz: *A Social History of American Technology*. New York: Oxford University Press, 1996.

Dahlquist, A. : *Megasthenes and Indian Religion*, Uppsala, 1960.

Dalton, Dennis : *Gandhi's Power : Nonviolence in Action*, New Delhi, OUP, 2001.

Eldridge, P.J.: *The Politics of Foreign Aid in India*, New York, Schocken, 1970.

Farquhar, J.N.: *Modern Religious Movements in India*, Munshiram, New Delhi, 1967.

Frauwallner, E..: *History of Indian Philosophy*, Motilal, Delhi, 1973.

Grisenold, H.D.: *Insights into Modern Hinduism*, Oxford, New York, 1934.

Gupte, Pranay: *Mother India: A Political Biography of Indira Gandhi*, New York, Scribner's, 1992.

Heinsath, Charles: *Indian Nationalism and Hindu Social Reform*, Princeton University Press, Princeton, 1964.

Hoerder, Dirk: *Cultures in Contact: World Migrations in the Second Millennium*. Durham, N.C.: Duke University Press, 2002.

Kaushik, Asha : *Globalization, Democracy and Culture : Situating Gandhian Alternatives*, Jaipur, Pointer, 2002.

Kranzberg, Melvin; and Carroll W. Pursell: _Technology in Western Civilization_, New York: Oxford University Press, 1967.

Maheshwari, Shriram: _Rural Development in India: A Public Policy Approach_, New Delhi, Sage, 1995.

Margarette Lincoln: _The Worlds of the East India Company_. Rochester, NY: Brewer, 2003.

Nanda, B. R. : _Gandhi and His Critics_, Oxford University Press, Delhi, 1993.

Pandey, B.N.: _The Break Up of British India_, London, Macmillan, 1969.

Parker Geoffrey, _Empire War and Faith in Early Modern Europe_,Penguin Books, London 2003.

Parnwell, Mike: _Population Movements and the Third World_, London: Routledge, 1993.

Porter, Andrew: _Oxford History of the British Empire: Nineteenth Century_, Oxford and New York: Oxford University Press, 2001.

Sturdy, David, _Fractured Europe, 1600-1721_, Blackwell, Oxford 2002.

Tallet, Frank, _War and Society in Early Modern Europe 1495–1715, Routledge, London 1992_.

Tomlinson, B. R.: _The Economy of Modern India, 1860–1970_, New York, Cambridge University Press, 1993.

Townsend, Charles: _The Oxford History of Modern War_ Oxford: Oxford University Press, 2000.

Varma, R.S.: _Bureaucracy in India_, Bhopal, Progress 1973.

Vohra, Ranbir: _The Making of India: A Historical Survey_, Armonk, M. E. Sharp, 1997.

Wainwright, A. Martin: _Inheritance of Empire: Britain, India, and the Balance of Power in Asia, 1938-55_, Praeger Publishers, 1993.

Warmington, E.H. : _The Commerce between the Roman Empire and India_, Cambridge, 1928.

Zaidi, A. Moin: _Evolution of Muslim Political Thought in India_, New Delhi: S. Chand, 1975-79.

Index

❑❑❑